FISH & DIVE

THE

CARIBBEAN

Vol. 1

A Candid Destination Guide
to the Bahamas, Bermuda, Jamaica, British Virgin
Islands, Cancun, Cozumel, Cayman Islands,
U.S. Virgin Islands and others

by

Larry Larsen and M. Timothy O'Keefe

Book 1 In The Outdoor Travel Series
by Larsen's Outdoor Publishing

ISBN 0-936513-17-9

Library of Congress 91-76441

Published by:

LARSEN'S OUTDOOR PUBLISHING
2640 Elizabeth Place
Lakeland, FL 33813

Senior Editor: Lilliam Morse Larsen

PRINTED IN THE UNITED STATES OF AMERICA

1 2 3 4 5 6 7 8 9 10

CONTENTS

ACKNOWLEDGEMENTS

I owe a tremendous debt of gratitude to 'Uncle' Don Stewart who restored the fun in diving when I started to burn out. Also to Ed Montague of Aqua-Field Publications and Marcella Martinez representing the Caribbean Tourism Organization, both for helping me to realize some of my dream trips. A special thanks is due to Mary Fazulak and American Airlines, who graciously provided transportation for most of my island trips and served as my lifeline to the Caribbean.

Special thanks are also due Marla Weech of Orlando, FL; Charlanne Fields of Wilson, NY, Winston-Salem, NC, and other points south; and Lisa Gibbons of Gallows Bay, St. Croix, for their invaluable assistance as underwater models and whose beauty you see gracing these pages.

M. Timothy O'Keefe

I wish to thank those charter captains and guides around the Caribbean who spent time showing me the best of their waters. I owe a special debt of gratitude to Captain Billy Black of Walker's Cay and Captain James Roberts, formerly of the "Renegade" for their friendship and guidance in offshore fishing. I also very much appreciate the hospitality of Tom O'Connell of Dallas, TX, for many years the captain of the best offshore fishing team in the Atlantic and Caribbean, the "Texas Terrors."

Special thanks also go to Cayman Airways, Walker's International and Air Jamaica for their support, and to my wife, Lilliam, for her photography support and modeling expertise on many of my trips throughout the Caribbean.

Larry Larsen

PREFACE

Putting divers and anglers together in the same guidebook may seem a little like mixing oil and vinegar. You might be able to get the two together for a short time, but each will soon return to its own level: one above the water line, the other below it.

Traditionally, anglers and divers haven't had much to do with each other. Divers figured the anglers would catch the reef fish they had traveled so far to see, while the fishermen regarded divers as nuisances cluttering up their favorite fishing holes.

But that's changing as more divers are now starting to devote time to catching fish instead of just watching them. As for fishermen, most of them have been snorkelers all along and many have become certified divers.

Even hard-core divers are finding they have more in common with line fishermen than they realized, that stalking fish on top of the water can be as much fun as finding them below. This new activity to fill time between dives is particularly appealing to veteran divers who've been looking for something in addition to-- not in place of--their diving while on vacation. If you use up all your bottom time on deep morning dives, fishing is the perfect way to spend the rest of the day.

The most environmentally-conscious diver should have no problem with this blending. Neither trolling offshore for big game fish like marlin and sailfish, nor poling over barren sand flats for bonefish, disturbs the reef life divers travel so far to see. Furthermore, catch-and-release is the dominant philosophy in Caribbean fishing these days. Some species, such as bonefish and permit, have never been kept anyway because they're considered inedible.

Furthermore, divers and anglers are the ones who are most likely to band together to conserve the marine resources in the islands.

For anyone who loves the water, we can think of no better places to spend a vacation than a fishing and diving trip to the Caribbean. You always have plenty to do, whether on or below the surface.

ABOUT THE AUTHORS

Larry Larsen

An angler for 40 years and certified diver for more than 20 years, Larry Larsen has traveled the Caribbean extensively in search of fishing and diving opportunities. His numerous articles and photos have appeared in over 50 regional and national outdoor and travel magazines. Larry is Florida Editor for *Outdoor Life*, and a frequent contributor to *Florida Sportsman, Saltwater Sportsman, Marlin, Sport Fishing, Southern Saltwater, Caribbean Travel & Life, Cruise Travel* and other major outdoor magazines. He is a member of the Outdoor Writers Association of America (OWAA), the Florida Outdoor Writers Association (FOWA) and the National Association of Independent Publishers (NAIP) and has been honored with many awards over the years for his writing, publishing and photography. Larry, holds a Master's from Colorado State University. He has authored 13 books on fishing and as President of Larsen's Outdoor Publishing, has published several additional outdoors titles.

M. Timothy O'Keefe

M. Timothy O'Keefe has been a diver and fisherman for more than 30 years. His articles and photos have appeared in many major publications, including National Geographic Society books, Time Life Books, *Travel & Leisure, Newsweek, Skin Diver, SCUBA Times, Caribbean Travel & Life, Saltwater Sportsman, Power & Motoryacht* and many others. He was editor of the first major dive travel guidebook published in the U.S., *The International Divers Guide* which described the best in diving worldwide, and was editor of *Diver's World*, the first newspaper published exclusively for divers. Tim holds a Ph D. from the University of North Carolina at Chapel Hill and is a professor in the School of Communication at the University of Central Florida in Orlando, where he established the journalism program. He is a member of the Outdoor Writers Association of America (OWAA) and the Society of American Travel Writers (SATW). His fishing and diving articles and photos have received numerous awards over the years.

INTRODUCTION

PRE-PLANNING FOR HASSLE-FREE CARIBBEAN TRAVEL

Sooner or later every saltwater angler and diver begins casting glances toward the far off horizons of the Caribbean. Thoughts of swaying palm trees and fish-filled crystal clear waters become almost obsessive.

The same question keeps recurring: "If other people can do it, why not me?"

Exactly. Why not you?

Traveling to the Caribbean is not much more difficult than journeying to another state. Just two or three hours will put you in the most remote regions. If you're flying to the Bahamas, you'll hardly have time to finish a soft drink before the plane starts descending.

One of the least considered--yet one of the most crucial-- elements is whether you've chosen the right time of year for your venture. Many people assume that it's warm, sunny and calm in the Caribbean year-round. After all, that's what the travel posters show, right? It's not so. In winter, cold fronts can play havoc in the Atlantic islands and even as far south as the Caymans. It gets cold and windy, and in extreme situations, it's possible that boats might not even be able to go out.

You need to consider carefully the weather patterns: the rainy periods, the hurricane season, plankton blooms, whatever. Nothing ruins a fishing or diving trip faster than lousy weather, and though you can't control it, you can minimize its effects according to the time of year you visit a particular locality. Once you've researched this aspect, you could well find the need to switch vacation schedules with a co-worker. That's a lot less aggravating than watching the winds howl while you chalk up expenses of $100-$200 per day sitting in an easy chair.

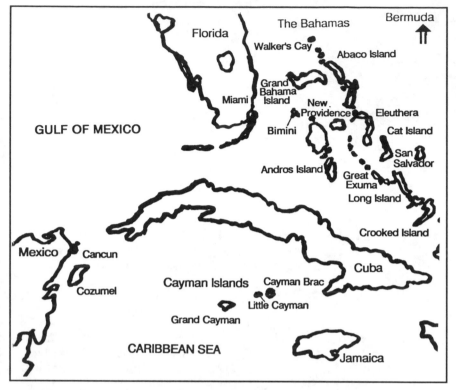

Because the Caribbean depends heavily on U.S. tourism, entry requirements to these foreign countries are minimal. Some islands don't even require a passport, only a valid voter's registration card and your picture on a driver's license. The U.S. Virgin Islands and Puerto Rico, essentially kissing cousins to the mainland, don't require even that.

However, passports are either required or a good idea for Bermuda, the BVI's, Mexico, Jamaica, Turks & Caicos, and the Cayman Islands. New passports take 5-6 weeks to arrive from the time an application goes in; passport offices are listed in the phone book in the U.S. Government section. Passports cost about $35 and last 10 years. No matter where you are, always keep close guard of your passport. As for proof of vaccination and other health information, it's not needed in the Caribbean, though it is a good idea to make sure your tetanus and typhoid shots are up to date for foreign travel anywhere.

Two aspects in particular of foreign travel tend to cause most problems. One is the loss of the immigration form you fill out

ATLANTIC OCEAN

Providenciales

Turks & Caicos

Great Inagua Island

British Virgin Islands

Tortola   Virgin Gorda

St. Thomas

Peter Island

Haiti

Dominican
Republic

St. John

U.S. Virgin Islands

Puerto Rico   St. Croix

when you enter another country. A copy of this form must be surrendered when you depart. If you lose it, immigration officials may put you through so much red tape your plane may leave without you. If you discover the form is missing, arrive at the airport early to plead your case.

An even worse problem is losing your return plane tickets. Because reconfirming flights is no longer standard practice in the States, many first-time travelers don't bother to reconfirm in the Caribbean although some airlines say you must. Since it's standard practice for airlines to overbook flights, you can bet money on losing your seat if you don't reconfirm as specified. Most carriers request reconfirmation at least 72 hours before departure. Best time to reconfirm is when you first arrive, since it's easy to get totally caught up in the fishing and diving and forget.

Another way to forfeit your return seat is through some sort of trip interruption. For instance, if you don't fly exactly as ticketed--if one flight is late and you're forced to change to another airline--your original carrier probably will dump your reservations

11

from its computer. Therefore, inform your airline immediately of any deviations from your ticketed schedule. It's more important to be on the passenger list than to have a ticket in hand.

Once you've arrived at your foreign destination, gone through customs and immigrations, the next step is to visit the airport bank for some local currency. Banks typically give better rates (sometimes as much as 3-5 percent better) than hotels will. Don't change dollars at airport banks in the U.S. That may seem convenient, but the service charge is stiff and the exchange rate often is not as good as at your destination.

Any leftover foreign currency at the end of your trip should be converted back to dollars at a bank either the evening before or the same morning you leave for home, keeping enough foreign money for airport departure tax and cab fare. Don't rely on the airport bank for this last transaction. Their hours are more accommodating to incoming than outgoing travelers.

Before departing the U.S., it's a good idea to have some sort of insurance to cover your luggage and contents. Your homeowners or tenants policy may already protect you; if not, purchase extra baggage insurance at the airport or through a travel agent.

You also need to ascertain the electrical current in the country you're visiting. If it's 220 volts, you will require a special transformer as well as an adaptor to use your rechargeable strobes, hair dryers or any other appliances safely. Those transformers are available only at electrical supply stores in the U.S.

Also, don't forget to register all your foreign-made items--especially cameras and radios--with U.S. Customs before you depart. Customs has a simple form you must fill out before you leave in order to avoid paying duty on imported articles when you return. You must show the Customs people any equipment you intend to register, so don't pack it away where you can't get to it.

Trip Planning

Your fishing or diving trip needs to be well remembered, but not for all the wrong reasons. Too many people believe all you need do is pack your gear carefully and you're guaranteed a good time. If that were true, people would never return home disappointed.

Planning a successful fishing or diving vacation requires extensive research and consideration of a wide range of contingencies. Choosing the right location is critical if you're not to be disappointed. Because of the large number of factors that crop up in making such a decision, it's not as easy as it might seem.

For instance, what kind of fishing or diving do you most want to do? What is the one thing you want to see or do on this trip that you've never experienced before? Are you most interested in photographing or studying marine life, or do you want to prowl the remains of as many shipwrecks as you can? Are you interested primarily in billfish or would you like to explore some bonefish flats as well?

Another factor to consider is just how much time you have for such a trip. Can you set aside two full weeks of vacation, or are you confined to a week or less, such as a long holiday weekend?

Finances are another important problem you must face honestly. Can you really afford to fulfill your Caribbean fantasy? If you think so, are you sure you know all the charges you're likely to encounter? It's surprising how many anglers and divers don't anticipate all costs before they depart.

For example, are you certain about what the cost of meals will run? In the Caribbean, many hotels routinely charge $20 to $30 for dinner, and you may not have anywhere else to dine. A week of such expenses for two--if not anticipated--can be financially disastrous.

Are there any hotel service charges or special taxes? Some resorts add a 10-15 percent service charge as a standard part of the bill. That adds up to a bit of change over an extended period of time. On top of the service charge, there may also be an additional government tax of 5-10 percent. Combined, these two "extras" can inflate your bill another 25 percent more than what you budgeted for. And, not all hotels accept credit cards, so you may need to pay in travelers checks.

Another point to ponder: do you get seasick easily? If so, avoid those places that specialize in long boat trips to their fishing or diving sites. It's different at each location, and you need to understand all your options before making a final decision.

If you're traveling with family members, do they all want to fish or dive as much as you do? If not, what other activities can they enjoy? It's possible there won't be any. Sometimes, the better the sportfishing or the diving is, the more remote the location. And the more remote the location, the less there is to do but fish or dive. If extensive shopping and an active night life are necessary to keep everyone happy, your destination options become more narrow.

Selecting a Dive Destination

Most places specialize in a certain type of activity; there are few that can meet everyone's needs, so you must match your desires with what can realistically be offered. Don't expect people to go out of their way to cater to your whims; you'll be only one of many vacationers, and dive charters are geared to satisfying the largest numbers, not the single few.

If underwater photography is your primary interest, obviously you'll need to select a spot with good visibility and abundant sea life. If wrecks are your thing, you're more apt to end up in an area swept by winds and turbulent waters, and where photography will be more difficult. If spearfishing is foremost on your agenda, you can just about forget foreign travel and plan on staying at home. Most popular dive destinations ban spearing, since the fish life is one of the primary reasons people visit.

Other points to consider: Do you and other accompanying members of your family have the experience to be able to dive the different sites a place has to offer? There's no sense in choosing a location where you'll frequently encounter currents and be making deep dives if you or a member of your family is still a novice. You won't be comfortable and you won't enjoy it.

Do you prefer beach or boat diving? Do you want to spend more time snorkeling than scuba diving? Some sites that are great for scuba are lousy for snorkeling because the reefs start too deep to enjoy them from the surface.

How much do the dives cost? Is it cheaper to buy them as a package in advance or pay on an individual basis? But if you do sign up for a package in advance, you're limited to the services of one dive operation, which prevents you from striking out on your own unless the operator will give you a refund for unused dives.

Consider, too, the kind of hotel you want to stay at. Should it be one which is exclusively a dive resort, or would you be happier at a general hotel that offers diving via an arrangement with a dive operation situated off the premises?

If you want to spend your free time with people who have the same interests and who will be happy to swap tales of their own adventures for yours, you'll probably have a great time at a dive resort. However, if diving is only one of your reasons for visiting a particular place, you might prefer a more general hotel where you'll have a wider variety of subjects to talk about with other guests at breakfast and dinner. But you might also find it more difficult to make friends because of the greater diversity of interests.

Along this same line, would you be happier if you traveled with a group of people you already knew instead of joining a bunch of strangers? If a large dose of familiarity is what you require in an unknown locale, you'll probably feel most comfortable joining a trip offered by the dive shop you frequent at home. That way you know in advance who's going to be present and how compatible the group will be.

Naturally, the best way to learn about a place is talk to someone who's been there. If you're unable to find such a person through your local dive club or dive store, write to the resort and ask them to send some names of previous guests. Then give these former vacationers a call and ask what you need to know. Most people are very helpful as long as your questions are brief and to the point.

Also, read about your destination before departure in order to become thoroughly familiar with an area. Consult not only dive publications for descriptions of the underwater terrain but invest in general travel guides which will give you detailed points about a place, its people and their customs. The more you know in advance, the more you know what to plan for.

When packing time finally arrives, take all your own gear except for tank and weights, which are normally provided. Rental equipment is not as likely to be as new or well maintained as your own. Even if it is, it won't provide the same confidence, or psychological advantage, your own familiar equipment does.

Here's what your equipment list should include: regulator with pressure gauge; mask, fins and snorkel; extra mask and fin straps; buoyancy compensator; wetsuit (which may help you even in the tropics against coral, etc.); knife; dive watch; bottom timer; underwater light for night diving; gloves; decompression tables; a basic scuba manual for review.

The suitcase you use to transport your dive gear should have stout locks and hard sides in order to withstand abuse. Soft luggage often won't provide the kind of protection required to thwart clumsy baggage handlers.

Next to your dive equipment, the most important items to carry are remedies for various dive and travel-related ills. For sinus blockage or sticky ears, Sudafeds are widely used since they don't make you drowsy. Also pack some ear wax remover, swimmer's ear medication, sunscreen, Adolph's meat tenderizer for coral scrapes, diarrhea medicine and a simple first aid kit. It's surprising how often you're forced to serve as your own pharmacy because none of the supplies are available.

Planning A Fishing Expedition

Gamefish in the Caribbean must be in league with each country's tourist boards, since fall through spring generally is the best angling period everywhere. That's good and bad. There's nothing better than a Caribbean vacation in winter, but airline fares and accommodations are highest from December 15 to April

15, the most desirable time to visit the Caribbean. You can save as much as 30 percent if you book either side of this peak period, and still catch fish.

Fishing opportunities in the Caribbean are unlimited, ranging from a remote camp in the middle of nowhere to living it up at one of the finest resorts in the U.S. Virgin Islands. It all depends on your own inclinations, budget--and whether you're taking a non-fishing spouse along. Remote fish camps offer little to do but fish, and that could drive some women stir-crazy after the first day.

Packing for a Caribbean trip poses some interesting questions. Foremost is whether to take your own tackle. It depends, really, on what you'll be fishing for. Charter boats for offshore trolling supply rods, bait and lures. Most charter captains are also very savvy about the latest trolling techniques. Soft plastic heads are popular for billfish, through many boats still trail at least one or two natural baits like ballyhoo or mullet. If you have a favorite trolling lure, by all means bring it to see how well it works way down South. But remember, you may lose it to a blue-water battler.

Spinning tackle is usually the preferred equipment for most shallow water species. Although complete outfits may be available for loan, take your own gear for bonefish, permit or tarpon. You can never be sure of the quality of equipment that gets passed around frequently and serviced haphazardly.

The most important piece of equipment for flats fishing is a high performance reel with a steady, smooth drag and a capacity of at least 200 yards of line. When something like a bonefish or big tarpon is tearing off a hundred yards of line, a jerky drag will often bust the mono, which is heartbreaking. Never skimp when it comes to selecting a good reel; this is not a trip you'll soon to repeat.

For bonefish, take a light rod and 6- to 8-pound test line and a good assortment of 1/8 or 1/4-ounce pink or white jigs. Permit demand a slightly heavier rod and 8- to 10-pound test mono. Their favorite forage is small crabs, which some guides provide. Bonefish and permit rigs are almost interchangeable (and can be in a pinch), but tarpon need 15 to 20-pound test mono and a rod capable of handling up to one-ounce plugs.

Although resident species such as bonefish and permit usually can be taken year-round, the summer sun is more than most anglers can stand. Some bonefish lodges either close down then, offer cut-rate packages (some real bargains here) or cater to scuba divers.

Planning a successful fishing or diving vacation requires extensive research to choose the right location.

Fly fishermen definitely need pack complete outfits since fly fishing equipment is about as rare in the Caribbean as a 200-pound tarpon. Bonefish like a rapidly sinking fly with marabou or bucktail streamer in No. 6 to 1/0 hook sizes. Pink is usually the hot color, though white often works, too. Permit, often tough to take on a fly, need slightly larger hook size, No. 4, No. 2 or 1/0. Sinking pink shrimp, marabou streamer or small bucktails produce best.

Tarpon on a flyrod is an incredible, unforgettable experience. Tarpon come in all sizes, from 5-pound babies to 100+ pound monsters. Tarpon up to 15-pounds take a 3/0 hook. Between 15-40, try a 4/0. Above that, a 5/0--and a fast prayer when it strikes. Streamers in red and white, blue and white, and red and yellow are all good choices. For large tarpon, most experts recommend 12 inches of 80- or 100-pound mono tied to a 12-pound tippet to keep the fish from fraying the line.

It's inconvenient enough to have normal luggage lost or damaged; it's a disaster when it's your fishing tackle. Plano makes several models of rod cases which survive most baggage handlers. Use small locks and duct tape to secure all openings and potential openings. Otherwise, hand carry broken down rods placed in a protective (but not bulky) rod case. Use a size that will fit in an overhead rack, if possible. If it won't fit there, try the coat closet. If the stewardesses start giving you a rough time, appeal to the pilot. He has the final say about everything.

Rods aren't much good without reels, so carry them aboard your plane in a small sport bag or suitcase that will fit under the seat in front of you.

Other essential items to pack are polarized sunglasses (absolutely vital for flats fishing so you can spot the fish), plenty of sunscreen, and a wide brimmed hat, long pants and/or long sleeve shirt for even more sun protection. That Caribbean sun is a lot hotter than anything in the South, even Florida.

And don't forget a good camera with a good supply of film-- to record all the fish you're going to catch.

1

BLACKBEARD'S ISLANDS

The Bahamas were home to the Lucayan Indians when the Spanish conquistadors arrived in search of gold and other treasures. English settlers arrived some years later in search of religious freedom, and settled on Eleuthera, which means 'freedom' in Greek. The islands were also favorite destinations for pirates until the British appointed a Royal Governor who promptly cleared them out. Today, the signs of pirate lore can be visited at Blackbeard's Tower in Nassau, the capital of the Bahamas, where most of the islands' 210,000 inhabitants reside.

Located 35 minutes from Florida's East Coast and 2 1/2 hours from New York, the Bahamas is made up of more than 700 islands and cays. American, USAir, Delta and TWA bring most passengers from at least 15 major U.S. cities to Nassau and Freeport through Miami, Fort Lauderdale and West Palm Beach airports. AeroCoach and Chalk's International connect to Treasure Cay, North Eleuthera, Rock Sound, Bimini, and Walker's Cay. Walker's International also flies to Walker's Cay. Bahamasair schedules can be irregular and undependable.

U.S. citizens need proof of citizenship such as voter's registration card, notarized birth certificate or passport, and return ticket. The U.S. dollar is accepted everywhere at its value, so there's no need to change money. Major credit cards are widely accepted. You are limited to $400 of merchandise to take home duty-free, and there's a $5 departure tax.

Rental cars are available on several islands, but remember that driving in the Bahamas is on the left. Visitors can drive for three months without having to obtain a Bahamian license. However, drivers need to be very careful -- traffic may be heavy and disorganized.

Walker's Cay is one of many secluded Bahamian hideaways.

Winter temperatures range from 68 F to 78; summertime is 76 F to 88 F. As with most islands, November through April is the busiest, and often more expensive, season. Geographically, the Bahamas are spread out in an arc over 750 miles long, and weather patterns differ from the northern end to the southern tip of the arc.

Activities are as varied as there are islands in the Bahamas. From the casinos and night life of Nassau and Freeport to the hideaways on remote islands like Walker's Cay. The glitz and glitter of Nassau and Freeport can overwhelm vacationers, but do take time to do some shopping where available. In Freeport, the Garden of the Groves and the International Shopping Bazaar are must-sees. In Nassau, visit Bay Street's shops and big straw market.

The "family" of islands (Abaco, Andros, Bimini, Eleuthera, Exuma) and half a dozen others have their own distinct personality. Some of the smaller cays are completely uninhabited, which is why sailboat or motorboat rentals are very popular here.

Andros, the largest Bahamian island, features the second largest barrier reef in the world. Bimini is often referred to as the Big Game Fishing Capital of the World. On Eleuthera, the rich blue of the Atlantic and the calm green waters of the Caribbean are separated only by a strip of rock. Exuma boasts the National Land and Sea Park, a vast underwater preserve.

Bahamas Tourism has made it easy to gain information. There are Bahamas Tourist Offices located in Atlanta, Boston, Charlotte, Chicago, Dallas, Detroit, Houston, Los Angeles, Miami, New York, Philadelphia, San Francisco and Washington, D.C. For general information, call 800/327-0787. For diving or sportsfishing information, call 800/32SPORT.

2

NORTHERN ABACO CHARM

Larry's Close Encounters With Big Game At The Top Of The Bahamas

The "relaxed little island" of Walker's Cay is the northernmost angling outpost in Abaco, Bahamas. A lot of excitement lies in the deep blue waters just north of the bank that stretches along the Abaco chain of islands...for those willing to risk sore backs and arm muscles.

The 100-acre spit of land is a real tropical "oasis" that has two swimming pools, a beach for shelling and snorkeling, shuffleboard, tennis, volleyball and horse shoes. A very comfortable and modern hotel and restaurant provide great accommodations and outstanding food. There are no phones or television to distract from the activities at hand.

The pristine waters at the so-called "Top of the Bahamas" offer anglers a great battle with virtually any of their favorite big game. It's easy to see why the area is renown for its offshore trolling for billfish and other big game angling opportunities. There is plenty of food for predators of all sizes. Several miles of fish-laden flats and shallow reefs surround Walker's, but to the north of the island, the depths drop off quickly.

Within two miles are 3,000-foot depths, and within another couple of miles 5,000 foot depths are the norm. That blue water runs the eastern side of the Abacos, and fish can be caught all along it. To find the best spots, though, the angler/boat captain needs to understand the current.

"The current normally runs north from the island through those waters," says Captain Billy Black whose 50-foot "Duchess" is

21

headquartered at Walker's. "Much of the action lies off the area between Matanilla Shoal, 12 miles west of Walker's Cay, to Stranger's Cay 20 miles to the east."

The "Duchess" is part of the island's year around fleet, along with three 23-foot Makos and a 45-foot sportfishing cruiser. The charters are often kept busy throughout the year chasing after blue marlin, kingfish, wahoo, grouper, dolphin, amberjack; any combination is a typical half-day catch. Big wahoo, a couple of 50-pound yellowfin tuna, some giant dolphin and a big blue marlin are often brought into the dock.

Walker's Sea Lion Marina

In my several visits to Walker's, the seas have been four to five feet. Trolling the outer banks, our surface baits skittered over 600 feet of blue water. The plastic lures of varying sizes on the 50 to 80 pound test lines seemed to dig into the waves and 'kiss' the surface only every five or six seconds. That was ideal, according to Black.

The weather was typical of winter, and not what we had hoped for. Four-foot swells were still appearing after a cold front that had kept us landlocked for two days. Billy, considered one of the top captains in the world, has caught blue marlin under similar circumstances, but it generally requires more effort. He slowed down the diesels and began to carefully watch the lures.

The captain, with over 350 blue marlin to his credit and several records for billfish, analyzed the seven baits we were trolling. Adjustments were made to stagger the various lures properly on the wakes, 50 to 200 feet behind the cruiser. It wasn't long before a 20 pound dolphin provided a tussle and anticipated "vittles" for the evening meal, and then came more waiting.

"Fish on!" Black suddenly yelled, as line started peeling from the reel, but we soon realized the foe was not the marlin we were seeking. Shortly afterwards, a 40-pound wahoo complemented our plans for dinner that night.

The wahoo off Walker's hit in the fall, winter and spring, and many are much larger than the one we landed. Black's largest weighed 113 pounds, but several he has caught also ran as large as 90 pounds. The captain recommends using 500 pound monofilament leader when the wahoo are abundant, which is often off the Northern Abacos. The fierce fish will cut 400 easily.

We again positioned our lures and began crisscrossing north of Walker's along the Bank. The fishing out front is some of the best in the Bahamas, according to Black.

"The wall off Walker's Cay is one of the best anywhere," he says. "The bottom will drop from 900 to 1,500 feet as you move east

The "Duchess" is part of the island's year around fleet.

to west. The easterly current hits that bank and boils the water all the way to the surface. Bait fish tend to lay in that turbulent water which offers stirred up sediment for small squid and other items in the food chain."

Black offered us a rundown on the action in the Northern Abacos: The white marlin migrate through the Walker's area after the very cold weather, in February and March. Those are also good months for catching wahoo. April generally signals the beginning of great billfishing and top angling action for dolphin. An occasional white can be caught in the off-season, but blues are even more numerous.

As if to underscore his thoughts, a blue marlin suddenly hit the right flat line.

"Blue marlin!" yelled Billy as I jumped in the fighting chair and the mate quickly grabbed the rod to jam it into the gimbal. This was the moment we had been waiting for. Sure enough, a handsome blue began tail-walking the surface trying to break free as I put the pressure on. But this marlin was not to be mine. The battle was short-lived. As they often do, the marlin spit out the lure and disappeared into the depths.

Naturally, it was disappointing, and we couldn't help remember a similar event a few years ago on my first visit to Walker's Cay. With Black's movie camera churning and our 35mm still cameras

23

Giant tuna, like this island record, frequent the nearby northern bank.

clicking, a marlin of over 200 pounds was doing a wild dance on the ocean's surface at the end of the line. That blue threw the hook after tail-walking for a full minute or more. We had a second chance at a similar size blue and lost it. Two blues raised in two off-season trips with Black is not a bad average. In fact, that's pretty impressive.

"Winds out of the west or north will usually offer clean waters, while winds from a southern or eastern direction will make the mid-depth areas dirty," according to Captain Jerome Broz of Walker's Sea Lion IX charter. "There are lots of channels around here, and the predators will hang around them for the feast if the water is relatively clear."

Grand Key to the east has a lot of reefs and the fishing is very good for snapper and grouper there. As you move east southeast down the Abaco chain, billfishing is also superb near the Doublebreaster Keys; all along the barrier reef. A particularly popular place for anglers is Carters Key - the halfway point between Walker's and Treasure Key. Black often ventures to Carters at night for some deep jigging and swordfishing.

When the wind is out of the east southeast, Grand Key is a relaxing place to catch a bonefish, behind the island on the lee. When the wind is from the north, it's better between the two islands Little and Big Grand Key, called bonefish flats on the charts. Great Seal, 20 miles away, also has good bonefishing.

The Serenades just south of the markers, and any shoal along the south side, are very productive for yellowtail; or, on the north side of the reefs if the wind is right at 100 to 200 feet, it's excellent for deep jigging for grouper or trolling for wahoo and kingfish. Mantanilla 12 miles away is also good. As is often the case, the further you get from the more populated and fished areas, the better it gets.

The Walker's Marina facilities equal any in this island nation; many Floridians keep their sportfishermen here and fly over on weekends. The Walker's Cay Resort will remind you a bit of the best hotels back home, only none of them will ever match the fine setting. Facing the open Atlantic, the waters around Walker's can get quite rough in winter.

For further information, contact Walker's Cay Hotel and Marina, 700 S.W. 34th Street, Ft. Lauderdale, FL 33315 or phone toll free 800/327-3714. In Florida call 800/432-2092.

3

ANDROS ISLAND BONEFISH

Some Of Tim's Favorite Bonefish Flats Are Virtually Unexplored

Earl Waters is out of the boat again, doing what he seems to do best: unlooping fly line that a bonefish has twisted around a hoard of mangrove roots.

Getting snarled seems to be a favorite habit of Andros Island bonefish, since this is the second one that's played loop-de-loop with Earl's line before speeding off into deep water. Last time Earl was lucky and saved his fish, but he'd happily trade it for this one, an exceptional bonefish that looks well over eight pounds.

Earl finally frees the line, just in time to see it go slack. He immediately raises his rod tip and starts cranking. The line snaps taut and Earl is rewarded with the sound of his drag kicking in again. A few minutes more and Earl is scooping the bonefish out of the water and weighing it at the boat: it goes just over nine.

We'd taken a seven-pounder the day before -- not too shabby a showing for the Andros Island Bonefish Club, one of the most modern bonefish camps on the Bahamas' largest out island.

Andros has long been known for superb bonefishing, but accommodations have often been a problem. Typically, anglers have had to stay in small hotels in town and then be shuttled back and forth to their boats. The Andros Island Bonefish Club has helped solve that dilemma. Since it opened in March of '88, the Club has gained an international reputation, attracting such noted anglers as Lefty Kreh, A.J. McClane and Billy Pate. That in turn has brought in fishermen from all over the country.

Bahamian Rupert Leadon is the Club's owner and chief guide. Although his facilities are relatively new, the experience of Rupert and his fellow guides is not. Rupert has guided the Andros area for almost two decades, which gives him an intimate knowledge of fish movements here. Most of his guides also have spent extensive time on the flats.

Andros Island flats are blessed with a lot of bonefish, big and small. While the average bonefish is around 5 pounds, lots of larger fish have been seen and taken.

Biggest for the Club is a 14-1/2 pounder, although one that probably weighed well over 16 pounds also has been landed. Its true weight couldn't be verified because a shark ate the tail section. Rupert says several people have spotted bonefish over 18 pounds, but so far no one has managed to entice these heavyweights.

Rupert believes some of these fish should have been caught, but his anglers just weren't up to it. The problem, he says, is that too many fishermen lack the ability to cast a fly far enough to reach the big fish.

"Eighty percent of the anglers who come here fly fish, but some of them shouldn't," Rupert says. "They can cast only 15-20 feet, but they refuse to use spinning.

"The big bonefish are too spooky to get so close. You need to be able to cast at least 60 feet to have any chance to reach these big fish. If you shove a boat in any closer, the fish will leave."

Andros Island Bonefish Club is located on Cargill's Creek in the upper northeast corner of the Andros Bights. The North Bight, a long wide expanse of alternating flats, rocks and cays, is right at the lodge's doorstep. Winding our 16-foot Dolphin Super Skiff through this maze, we always found a lee shore regardless of wind direction.

One of the most popular spots is known as Spanish Wells. The channel leading to the mud-bottomed flat is deep and the sides incredibly straight. It looks man-made, but our guide Glister swore it was a natural phenomenon. After all, who would dig a channel out in the middle of nowhere?

Only someone who knows how much bonefish would appreciate such a deep hole. Bonefish head there at low tide, then re-emerge onto the huge mud bottom flat. It's a good cool hiding place for summertime. The deep hole also is where every hooked fish automatically goes, unless of course it detours to shore to first wrap itself around a few mangroves as ours did. When we fished here, we tried to take advantage of the channel refuge by placing our boat between it and the fish.

Andros Island flats are blessed with a lot of bonefish, big and small. While the average bonefish is around 5 pounds, lots of larger fish have been seen and taken.

Our first Spanish Wells bonefish taught us an important lesson about how the fish here generally feed. Unlike Keys bones, Andros fish do not favor a fast retrieve. In fact, they often run from it.

It was something that Glister kept trying to impress on us over and over that first morning. He kept urging, "Slow, down! Slow, down! These fish eat slow moving crustaceans, like small shrimp and crabs. They don't like to chase their food. You need to slow down!"

He was right, but old habits are hard to break. Only when we finally heeded his advice and reduced our retrieve almost to a crawl did the bonefish show any interest. Their forage may move slowly, but they certainly don't, not once they feel the hook.

At least the bones weren't finicky about what lures they ate.

Flies and jigs popular in the Keys work equally well here. For fly fishing, that includes No. 4 pink or brown Crazy Charlies, Orange Mite Mites and Epoxy Charlies. Seven to 9 weight rods with matching floating line, a reel with a capacity of at least 150 yards of backing, tippets of 8 or 10 pounds and 9 feet of leader are the preferred setups. For spinning, 1/4 oz wiggle jigs in brown and white, yellow or pink all produce equally well.

A couple of other quick comparisons between Andros and the Keys. Andros bonefish aren't nearly as spooky since they don't have that many people chasing them. And the Andros flats are far more extensive. Most fishing is done over a clear bottom and not grassy areas which predominate in parts of the Keys.

Besides a slow retrieve, another important point we quickly learned about Andros was the importance of the moon on fishing. If at all possible, avoid a full moon. Unfortunately, we didn't. Full moon conditions all favor the fish: lots of wind (bad enough) but also many cloudy days. As Rupert says, "Clouds take away 90 percent of the fishing."

A full moon also brings higher tides, which allow fish to stay back in the mangroves where we sometimes couldn't reach them. When we did, we had to fight to keep them from going back in. Three weeks out of the month, a lot of the mangrove cays we found awash would normally be high and dry.

Earl and I also were fishing in the hot days of July. Obviously, we found good numbers of big fish, but we didn't see great rafts of fish that Andros is noted for. According to Rupert, February and March are when he sees the most fish. Bonefish move in on the flats then to feed before and after the spawn.

That puts them in a more voracious mood than our hot weather July bones who seemed to lose interest in eating as the water warmed up near mid-day. They often stopped feeding completely, until late afternoon when the flats began to cool down.

Although Spanish Wells' soft muddy bottom made walking difficult, we found many areas that had a packed sand bottom ideally suited for wading. We tried this method several times but without a great deal of success. Once, a large school of fish that we stalked relentlessly for over an hour stayed just out of effective casting range. In frustration we finally tossed our lures near the school, and as a single unit they reacted by swimming away instantly.

Fishing the bights, we saw plenty of bonefish but none of the permit or tarpon that also inhabit Andros. Rupert thought we might see a better variety if we fished farther north in Stafford Creek. We'd fish in the creek bays early in the morning, then work our way out toward the flats nearest the ocean.

It's easier to reach Stafford Creek by car, so we trailered the boat for 45 minutes back toward Andros Town. Before this road was paved about a decade ago, it took three hours to travel the 30 miles to the airport there. Now it only takes a half hour. Not all progress is bad.

Stafford Creek turned out to have a fairly hard bottom in many sections, quite different from the bights' flats. We fished a perfect tide but the fish were amazingly few. When we did encounter them, we tried to cast to a specific fish rather than to the whole school. Smaller fish are usually more aggressive, and the surest way to take a larger fish is to cast specifically to it. Casting into the middle of a big school sometimes will spook the whole lot.

Rupert has excellent eyesight, but we did our best to spot fish as well. That gave our boat six eyes instead of just a single pair. A couple of times we actually did see a fish before Rupert.

After landing several fish in the creek, we headed out the channel toward the ocean. High wind kept us from venturing out as far as we would have liked. The flats there are incredibly beautiful, that alternating blend of white sand bottom, bright turquoise and deep channel blue. We took several good fish there, including the 7-pounder who struck just before it started to rain.

If at all possible, anglers should avoid using the services of Bahamasair and arrange a charter from Miami or Ft. Lauderdale. Our Bahamasair flight from Nassau to Andros Town, a mere 20 minute hop, was over four hours late arriving. That was an unusually long delay, but Bahamasair is notorious for not keeping a schedule. As the locals say, "Fly Bahamasair only when you have time to spare."

Roundtrip transportation and Club reservations can be made through World Wide Sportsman, P.O. Drawer 787, Islamorada, FL 33036; phone 305/664-4615 in Islamorada. In Miami call 305/238-9252. Outside Florida call toll free 800/327-2880.

Good luck on staying out of the mangroves.

4

FISHING VARIETY

A Roundup Of Fishing Opportunities Fishing licenses are not required by saltwater anglers, but visiting boats must buy a permit before anyone aboard may legally fish. Cost is $10 for a single visit or $50 for an annual permit. The permit allows only hook and line and up to six rods per boat and is easily obtained at any of the ports of entry. Other restrictions include six kingfish, dolphin and wahoo, or a combination of these species, per person on the boat. Capturing or killing turtles is prohibited. The lobster season is August through March, and limits are six per person, measuring at least 3 3/8 inches long or having a six-inch tail.

Billfish cannot be brought into the U.S., not even for mounting, unless they meet minimum size requirements of 57 inches for sailfish, 62 inches for white marlin and 86 inches for blue marlin. Heavyweights like marlin and tuna have made the Bahamas world famous, but they are just a sampling of the variety available: barracuda, bonefish, bonito, sailfish, mackerel, dolphin, grouper, wahoo, tuna, shark and swordfish all roam the Bahamas' crystal clear waters.

The Bahamas is one place where you truly can have it all: trolling offshore, stalking shallow water flats and reef fishing. Best of all, the different types of angling are usually available in just one location.

The real problem is deciding which island to use as your base. Although hundreds of islands make up the Bahamas chain, only a relative few have developed the fishing facilities that serious anglers look for. That's something of a blessing since the decision is difficult enough already.

Following are the major islands (other than Walker's Cay and Andros) and the kinds of action/facilities you can expect to find there.

Grand Bahama/Nassau

Located just 60 miles from the Florida coast, Grand Bahama Island is perhaps the best spot for good fishing while enjoying prime luxury. At West End there's the Grand Bahama Hotel and Marina with a good selection of charters for offshore, bonefishing and reef fishing. The hotel also has a championship golf course and nightly entertainment and regular shopping trips into the Bahamas second largest city, Freeport/Lucaya.

Freeport/Lucaya itself has excellent charter facilities and certainly the island's most luxurious hotels, such as the Xanadu Beach Hotel where reclusive millionaire Howard Hughes spent his final years. Two convenient hotels include the Holiday Inn and the Atlantik Beach Hotel. The only problem with Freeport is it has a lot of big city bustle and a less friendly attitude on the part of some locals; things are more serene at West End.

At the tip of Grand Bahama's East End is the famous Deep Water Cay Club. This is not a fish camp in the traditional sense but very comfortable, semi-luxury living. Located on its own island, the Club offers miles of winding channels and flats for bonefish. In May, bonefish stack up like cordwood in some sections apparently as part of the breeding ritual. Trips for truly mammoth permit between 30 to 50 pounds can be undertaken in calm weather.

Nassau/New Providence is the playground of the Bahamas and the ideal compromise location for a non-fishing spouse. Unfortunately, and as to be expected in such a populated area, the fishing isn't as good as many of the other places mentioned. Good charter facilities, though, that seek out sails in the fall, wahoo in the winter and marlin year-round. Bonefishing and reef fishing is below par compared to many other locations. But for things to do off the water, Nassau can't be beat: gambling, night club revues, beautiful white sand beaches and a plethora of shops. Like Freeport, this is a big city with all the hustle and bustle. But from the non-stop flow of tourists, obviously a lot of people like it.

Treasure Cay/Chub Cay

Part of the Abacos chain, Treasure Cay has come into real prominence in recent years as another top-notch billfishing center to rival Walker's. Bonefishing also can be quite good. Across the channel from Treasure Cay is picturesque Green Turtle Cay, a

From late April to November, permit prowl the deeper Bahamian flats, usually falling in the 5 to 20 pound category.

Bahamas version of a New England fishing village. A very quiet, quaint small island, the boats here fish the same waters as Treasure Cay although Green Turtle probably has better bonefishing flats and the fish are larger.

Another world famous billfishing area, Chub Cay owes its productivity to the "Pocket" or Northwest Channel that funnels deep into the shallow Bahamas Bank. Blue marlin are plentiful, but it's their smaller cousin, the white marlin, that really gets the reels singing in spring. The numbers of dolphin can be incredible, enough reason to pack a couple of light spinning rods for the schoolies that surround a boat once a single fish is hooked.

Boats headquartered here also have several other deep water regions to choose throughout the Berry Islands, of which Chub is a part. Bonefishing usually gets short shrift because of the concentration on offshore species, but the fish can be found patiently waiting close by. Another unique feature here is the chance for small tarpon, very unusual for the Bahamas.

The Family Islands

Just 50 miles from Florida, Bimini is the closest island to the mainland. Situated where the Gulf Stream meets the Bahamas Banks, Bimini is the revered big-game fishing capital of the Bahamas, holding both the blue marlin record (over 1,000 pounds) and the bonefish record (16 pounds). Several bones of 15 pounds also have been caught in recent years.

Bimini bonefish and blue marlin have no real season but are taken anytime. White marlin run strongest from January to May. Wahoo and giant tuna are most plentiful in winter months, with dolphin peaking in spring. Unfortunately, the legendary days of the giant bluefin tuna are over for the present since the species has been in general decline. Bimini offers several places to stay, including the Blue Water Ltd. Resort and the famous Bimini Big Game Club.

Great Exuma, home to the Out Island Inn, is another prime bonefish and permit location. Bones average 3 to 5 pounds and occasionally even trophies over 10 are hooked, so the fish are a quality size. Best weather condition for locating the fish is from late April to November. During the same period, permit prowl the deeper flats, usually falling in the 5 to 20 pound category. Resort facilities include tennis courts, a swimming pool and a private beach.

Migratory species including billfish favor the submerged ridge that juts from the ocean floor to within a hundred feet of the surface in the Cat Island/Eleuthera area. This ridge runs from the north end of Cat Island to the southern tip of Eleuthera. Eleuthera enjoys a second 17-mile long ridge formation extending from its northern tip, where depths drop sharply from 14 to 403 fathoms. Bonefishing and reef fishing on Eleuthera are also quite good.

5

DIVING WITH DOLPHINS
AND SHARKS

**Where
Tim
Swims
With His
Favorites:
Dolphins
And
Sharks**

The Underwater Explorers Society (UNEXSO) in Freeport has two of the Caribbean's most unusual and exciting animal interaction shows, the dolphin experience and a shark feeding dive. It's not surprising UNEXSO is involved since it runs the best equipped dive facility in the Western hemisphere.

Founded in 1965, UNEXSO boasts the kinds of equipment and staff that other operations can only dream of. With a staff of 50, UNEXSO has two training pools including an 18-foot deep tank with portals used for checking-out new arrivals and for training novices. Housing the Bahamas' only recompression chamber, it also contains a complete dive shop, classroom and library, four dive boats and a camera-video operation that surpasses anything I've ever seen.

The way UNEXSO videotapes its dives is a good illustration of the outfit's professionalism. The dive is taped in the normal manner, with the photographer unobtrusively accompanying every group. As soon as the boat returns to the dock, the tape of the just completed dive is shown in the camera store within five minutes. Naturally this is a good way to take orders for tapes while the enthusiasm is still hot, but it also shows how UNEXSO operates: getting a job well done with no messing around.

UNEXSO goes beyond swimming with dolphins in the confines of a pool. It takes its dolphins, a pair at a time, out into the open ocean where divers have the chance to feed, stroke and swim with the animals. This dolphin experience, costing about $100 per diver, is so popular that it's booked weeks in advance.

Trainer Mike Schultz originated the open release concept and designed the training, which began in February, 1987, after the five captured Atlantic bottlenose dolphin were airlifted from Mexico's Bay of Campeche. The dolphin, kept in a holding pen just to the right of the UNEXSO docks, had to be taught to follow Mike's boat to a particular reef area, then be persuaded to swim back to the holding pen. The tricky part of all this was that the dolphins could leave any time they wished. In fact, they still can.

The sides of the pens are just above water level, and at night the dolphin occasionally jump out, go exploring, and return before morning. Obviously, these animals are not being held against their will but stay because of the strong bond with their trainer and the ready food supply he provides.

Before each dolphin encounter, divers learn little-known details about dolphins, including a hydrophone demonstration with some of the dolphin sounds they will hear underwater. Most importantly, Mike instructs everyone on the different hand signals divers must use for the dolphin to behave properly. Remembering and using those hand signals are crucial to a successful dive.

In about 40 feet of water, divers kneel in a circle and take turns feeding fish from a large mesh sack that is slowly passed around the group. The dolphin, always eager for the offering, hover upside down in front of a diver for several minutes at a time before rocketing to the surface for a quick breath. Then they return to the same spot. Divers are encouraged to pet and stroke the animals, careful to avoid touching their eyes.

The dolphins' incredible energy makes it seem they're in non-stop motion, hyperactive creatures unable to pause for very long. This can make photography difficult if the dolphin stir up lots of sand. The best way to shoot the action is to photograph the divers on either side of you. If the bottom is stirred up, try standing and shooting down; there's usually less scatter at this height. Depending on how the dive is planned, you may not be able to move around much more than this.

After the dolphin have gone around the circle several times, divers float one at a time several feet off the bottom. At a signal from Mike, they firmly take hold of the dolphin's dorsal fin and the animal quickly swims to its trainer. While being pulled, divers also swim at the same time in order to keep the buckles on their equipment from bumping against the animal. The entire dive lasts a very fast 40 minutes.

"The Tears of Allah" is a 92-foot freighter intentionally sunk in 45 feet for a James Bond movie "Never Say Never Again."

The plastic head of a great white shark breaks through a wall of the Brass Helmet Restaurant located over the top of the UNEXSO dive shop, but Caribbean reef sharks in the flesh await at Shark Junction. Here divers line up with their backs against an old underwater habitat to avoid any possible surprises. Then the divemaster begins feeding 10-12 feet in front of the group.

Several large grouper and a frenzy of yellowtail snapper quickly snatch most of the food. If all goes as planned, the sharks show up about 15-20 minutes into the 40 minute dive. Some slowly laze their way over to the feeding while others stay just at the range of vision, apparently too timid to come in. With luck, as many as five sharks will appear. On the other hand, they may stay well away, never feeding once, or they may not show up at all.

When the sharks are active, Shark Junction is an exciting dive. When they're uncooperative, some people have almost fallen asleep underwater. There's just no predicting what will happen.

Of course UNEXSO offers lots of other dives (as many as three a day plus a night dive) on reefs and wrecks.

The crystal-clear waters of the Bahamas are ideal for snorkelers and divers of all skill levels.

Compared to Freeport, diving in Nassau is a relatively recent development. Its best diving is on the southwest coast of New Providence Island, normally protected from the prevailing winds. That's a long car ride from Nassau and its big resorts, but several shops do caravan guests out to the area daily.

Naturally, it's easier to be on location, something the Divi Bahamas Beach Resort and Country Club provides exceptionally well. Its setting is unusually elaborate for a dive resort: bordered by 1,500 feet of beach on one side and an 18-hole championship golf course on the other. As at other Divis, Peter Hughes is in charge of the well equipped, organized and efficient diving services.

Diving along the southwest coast can be unusually good because of the proximity of the Tongue of the Ocean, a 6,000-foot trench that brings clear water and big deep-water migratory fish close in. The vertical dropoffs tend to be spectacular, and they start as shallow as 40 feet.

The schedule for my recent visit called for a wall dive first followed by a shallow reef dive. Something that surprised me was how late the dive boats left. Accustomed to the normal island competition to get to sites first, Divi always appeared to be the last to arrive. But thanks to the constant current, I never had to follow in the wake and debris of the previous groups since evidence of their visit was washed away by the time we arrived.

Perhaps one disappointing feature was the afternoon dive, scheduled more for the convenience of snorkelers. Divers in the afternoon really had nothing to interest them. At one site, neither did the snorkelers, since the location contained mostly dead coral.

The southwest coast has been the location of many famous movies: "Thunderball," "20,000 Leagues Under the Sea," "For Your Eyes Only" and "Never Say Never Again." Several of the James Bond underwater film sets are close together. Oldest is the framework of a fake fighter plane which in "Thunderball" splashed down with a nuclear device aboard. The metal supports are loaded with gorgonians in many places, and you can usually find a couple of big fish if you're first inside. "The Tears of Allah" is a 92-foot freighter intentionally sunk in 45 feet for "Never Say Never Again." Goulding Cay's magnificent stands of elkhorn coral were featured in "20,000 Leagues," "For Your Eyes Only" and "Splash," so you know that has to be a pretty impressive spot.

For information on the Divi Bahamas, contact Divi Hotels, 54 Gunderman Rd., Ithaca, NY 14850; toll free at 800/333-3484 or 607/277-3484. UNEXSO is by far the best dive outfitter in Freeport. Call toll free 800/992-DIVE or 305/359-2730. Or write P.O. Box 5608, Ft. Lauderdale, FL 33310. Other good Nassau operations to try: Nassau Undersea Adventures, 809/362-4171; Dive Dive Dive, 809/362-1143; and Sun Divers, 809/325-8927.

6

DIVING THE LESSER-KNOWN ISLANDS

**The Best
Of The
Rest
In
Brief**

Walker's Cay is the northernmost Bahamian island, part of the Abacos chain. Like most of the islands in this region, diving is essentially patch reefs and coral heads in the shallows (usually inhabited by plenty of fish) and tall, narrow pinnacles in the deeper ranges.

There are not many places where snorkeling and diving can be combined as well as at Walker's Cay. The intricate coral heads come right up to the water's surface; snorkelers are comfortable going around the tops of the heads while divers can explore the 30 or 40-foot depths of the same heads. This island is particularly appealing to novice divers due to its shallow dive sites.

The island's dozen 'noted' dive sites are within a short boat trip, 10 to 20 minutes. Some of the named dive spots have revealed several old wrecks with cannons and other items from an old Spanish galleons and English war ships. Other reef sites offer a variety of fish life; at one we watched eagle rays do some incredible underwater ballet right in front of us. Tarpon are found on the shallow flats mostly, and there's one particular hole off the island where divers can consistently see five or six of the prehistoric-looking fish.

Diving to see sharks is getting popular, and one of the most interesting sites at Walker's is called the "zoo," because you never know what you'll see cruising by. Sometimes a hammerhead or bull shark will come along and check you out...and at the end of the dive, you swim into the shark canyons. For some reason, the sharks

The lobster season is August through March, and limits are six per person, measuring at least 3 3/8 inches long or having a six-inch tail.

like to hang out in these double canyons shaped in the form of a horseshoe.

Besides Walkers, there's popular diving at Treasure Cay, Marsh Harbour and Green Turtle Cay. Eels, grouper and rays are found in most locations, while the waters around Green Turtle Cay also hold the promise of spotting tarpon.

The Family Islands

Andros is the largest of all the islands and has one of the world's longest barrier reefs. Blue holes can also be found here, though they should be dived only with a knowledgeable guide. Not nearly as crowded as Nassau, the diving is far superior. Looking into the abyss known as the Tongue of the Ocean is an unforgettable experience.

The Berry Islands are composed of 30 islands in all, and Chub Cay features the renowned "fishbowl" usually filled with numerous grouper. Eagle rays, bottlenose dolphins and pilot whales are common diving companions. Bimini, also part of the group, is best known for its underwater phenomenon called the Bimini Road (called everything from a remnant of lost Atlantis to an extra-terrestrial landing site). The best diving is away from this notorious spot at some of the lesser known reefs and walls.

Eleuthera's Harbour Island and Spanish Wells contain some of the best diving along this vastly underrated island. Many of the better sites are shallow, from 30 to 40 feet, so bottom time can be considerable. Current Cut at the northern tip is known for its 6-8 knot current zips divers from one end of the cut to the other, where a dive boat awaits for pick up. This is perhaps the best drift dive anywhere in our hemisphere.

Hundreds of islands and cays make up the little-visited region of Exumas. Georgetown and Rum Cay are the best known spots. Rum Cay in particular is loaded with tame grouper that do their best to meet the demands of every visiting photographer.

Where Columbus supposedly first stepped on land after his sail over from Europe, San Salvador has been a favorite for serious divers for many years. The diving, day or night, is exceptional. Fish, corals and unusual forms of marine life--San Sal is a superb place to capture them all on a single trip.

7

TRIANGLE WRECKS

Tim Encounters The Real Bermuda Triangle -- On A Dinner Plate

Bermuda is an unusual place, and not just because of the legendary Triangle which carries its name. For one thing, Bermuda is not where most people expect to find it--somewhere near the Bahamas or deep in the Caribbean. Although Bermuda has the same rich foliage, gorgeous white sand beaches and warm summertime climate of the Caribbean, it's actually some 600 miles east of Cape Hatteras, N.C., kept warm year-round by the Gulf Stream.

Beautifully and painstakingly landscaped, Bermuda reflects its prosperity everywhere. The island, with its colorful flowers and striking pastel homes, looks like one vast estate.

Unfortunately, Bermuda not only looks expensive, it is. Prices generally are considerably higher than the Caribbean. Hotel dinners average $40-$50 a person with wine and tip, hotel rooms typically start at $150 a day, and taxi fares can be murderous--as much as $100 a if you want to explore thoroughly in a car rather than on a motorbike. (Rental cars are not available in order to keep down traffic congestion.)

In addition, for many years Bermuda was a cash-only society. Hotels and restaurants would not accept credit cards. That rather important detail sometimes came as an unpleasant surprise for some vacationers who ended up budgeting during their entire trip.

Dress is more formal than in many Caribbean islands. Men are expected to wear coats and ties and women to dress equally formally for dinner. Casual American-type attire is fine during the day, except that swim suits are never permitted in a dining room. Nor may gentlemen joggers run around without a shirt; it's a potential $100 fine if they do. Of course, men are permitted to wear their shorts to any formal occasion as long as they include coat and tie and have matching shoes and socks; after all, Bermuda shorts were born here.

Since Bermuda's proximity to the northeast made it both a convenient weekend retreat and a favorite spot for honeymooners of that region, it could well afford to rest on its popularity and reputation as a comfortable playground only for the well-heeled. However, increasing competition with other destinations has forced Bermuda to make some important concessions to attract visitors. For one thing, it's not a rude request if you ask to pay for your hotel room and restaurant charges with a credit card, though many stores and even some restaurants still refuse to accept them.

Actually, 150 different small islands make up what we call Bermuda, but the term usually refers only to the seven largest islands joined by bridges and causeways. These interconnected islands form the shape of a fishhook 22 miles long and only two miles across at the widest point. The 20 mph speed limit means it takes an hour to get from one end of Bermuda to the other. So, you might as well move at the same slow pace the islanders do; they even set the clock for ferry departures five minutes slow so latecomers won't miss the boat.

Probably the most interesting spot for sightseeing is the parish of St. George's at the eastern-most tip, the spot where in 1609 Admiral Sir George Somers, bound for the American colonies, ran his flagship "Sea Venture" aground. On Ordinance Island is a replica of the "Deliverance," one of two vessels fashioned out of the remains the wrecked "Sea Venture." Located nearby is the ducking stool once used on nagging wives and suspected witches. It's still employed every Wednesday when the St. George's town crier dunks a local volunteer, much to the delight of assembled tourists.

Replicas of the stocks, pillory and whipping post used to punish criminals 300 years ago are located in King's Square. Most of the people sticking their heads and arms through the devices today are honeymooners posing for a camera.

Hamilton Parish contains Bermuda's widest range of activities, ranging from traditional outdoor sports such as golf to spelunking and walking underwater. The Mid Ocean and Castle Harbour Golf Clubs are two of the finest golf courses anywhere. And the beautiful stalactites and stalagmites of the Leamington Caves and Crystal Caves can be stunning.

Many of the beaches are secluded by great rock formations that turn them into private coves.

But for many the odds-on favorite is the chance to walk on the ocean floor wearing a diver's helmet. You don't need to know how to do anything but walk and breathe in order to enjoy this unusual opportunity. The helmet dive takes place offshore in less than 12 feet of water. Divers stay within a limited area under the boat. Bronson Hartley originated the helmet dives many decades ago when he made all of his own equipment, well before the age of scuba. He still leads underwater trips every day from his operation in Flatts Village in Hamilton Parish.

Bermuda is a beach lover's paradise. The beautiful white sand beaches are used for almost everything--walking, swimming, jogging, horseback riding, snorkeling and just plain sunning. What's so nice is many of the beaches are secluded by great rock formations that turn them into private coves. Horseshoe Bay in Southampton is considered the most beautiful beach because of the brilliant color of the water and sand. Other standouts are West Whale Bay, Church Bay, Jobson's Cove and Warwick Long Bay, to name a few. You could go to a different spot each morning and still never see all the beaches, even during a two-week stay.

Besides its beaches, Bermuda is well known for its bargain shopping. The best selection is in the capital city of Hamilton on Front Street. Look for good buys in fine china, pottery, crystal, linen and imported clothing. The best bargains are woolen items from the British Isles -- at least 30 percent less than in the U.S.

One thing you don't find Bermudians much concerned about is their fearsome reputation as the apex of the notorious Bermuda Triangle. To amused islanders, the Bermuda Triangle is most familiar as a special dish consisting of a split broiled lobster that forms the top of the triangle, with a small beef fillet at the base.

American Airlines makes what is probably the shortest hop from its Raleigh-Durham hub. Its mid-day departure is an ideal time for most travelers since it provides connections from many other parts of the country. Delta and Air Canada also fly here. U.S. citizens need a passport, a voter's registration card or a birth certificate.

It may be a different color, but one Bermudian dollar equals one U.S. dollar. American money is accepted everywhere.

Contact the Bermuda Dept. of Tourism, Suite 201, 310 Madison Ave., New York, NY 10017; or call toll free 800/223-6106.

Shipwrecks Galore

Bermuda has two defined seasons, winter and summer. The islands are close enough to the States to be affected by our cold fronts in the winter, so avoid the island from November to May. The islands are also far enough in the Atlantic to enjoy subtropical weather in the summer, which means that wet suits are not needed during summer months. However, even in the summer strong winds will sometimes put the hiatus on diving for several days at a time. I've found September and early October, just after the high season is over, a fairly good weather time.

It's best to bring everything but a tank and weight belt. Water temperature can reach a bathtub 85-degrees in July, but wet suits may be needed at the beginning and end of the season.

The earliest sailors called Bermuda the "Isle of Devils" because its treacherous waters were such a menace to navigation. The protective barrier reefs killed over 500 vessels, depositing more shipwrecks on the ocean floor per square mile than anywhere else on earth.

Legends die hard, and today this same small island group forms the apex of our dreaded Bermuda Triangle, a zone in which planes as well as ships are said to disappear with terrible regularity. Bermuda's wreck-strewn waters do not appear to belie the modern myth.

However, what was the nightmarish misfortune for many a sailor is a wreck diver's dream. Most vessels are just off shore in shallow water, contain plenty of interesting remains, and are easily accessible during the summer months. But like the mysteriously abandoned ghost ship "The Mary Celeste," Bermuda's wrecks have been strangely devoid of divers.

The story of Bermuda diving is almost as curious as the Triangle legends. For a time, it was extremely fashionable to dive here; then--like the "Celeste's" doomed crew--divers virtually disappeared. That's an ironic turn of events, considering how Bermuda was a pioneer in sport diving.

Bermuda's shipwreck fleet also created some of diving's earliest treasure hunting excitement. The Mel Fisher of the 1950's was a fellow by the name of Teddy Tucker, who located millions on Bermuda's reefs. Despite this impressive heritage, as diving began to grow as a serious sport, Bermuda generally was by-passed in favor of islands farther south in the Caribbean. The reason?

"Bermuda simply was too expensive," says a long-time Bermuda divemaster. "It priced itself out of the diving market. But now that's changing. Divers are starting to come back because Bermuda's prices are getting more reasonable."

Several factors have helped make Bermuda more affordable now. One is the rising popularity of guest houses and condominiums as an alternative to the luxury hotels that average several hundred dollars a night. Further, airlines are promoting the air/land packages that the Caribbean has relied on for years.

Just as important, the dive operations are making more of an attempt to publicize their own involvement with certain hotels or guests houses. These links were not always obvious enough to prospective tourists or even newly arrived divers who often felt too much was required of them to make dive arrangements. As incredible as it may seem, in the 1970's when dive travel was booming, Bermuda had only two dive operators (not counting Bronson Hartley's helmet tours).

Today the number has tripled to six, yet the number may not grow significantly larger until Bermuda's officials decide to advertise their island as an important dive destination. That's something they may never need to do as long as honeymooners, golf enthusiasts, bargain shoppers and cruise ships keep coming in record numbers.

Bronson Hartley originated the helmet dives decades ago when he made all of his own equipment, well before the age of scuba. He still schedules daily trips from his operation in Flatts Village in Hamilton Parish.

Those who do come to see Bermuda's shipwrecks will discover an unbelievably idyllic situation. Diving is similar to the way the Caribbean was in the 1960's, when underwater swimmers were few, the sites uncrowded and undamaged, and divers were treated as individuals instead of cattle.

Bermuda's unusual geography and location are responsible for many shipwrecks that seemingly damned its reputation forever. Its location placed it in the middle of the route most ships followed between Europe and the New World. The invisible low-lying reefs, coming within inches of the surface, caught the ship captains by complete surprise: these are the most northerly coral reefs in the world.

Of Bermuda's many wrecks, about 30 are visited regularly. With the barrier reef coming is as close as 400 yards at the South Shore and extending as much as 12 miles out off the North Shore, running time varies between 10 to 90 minutes. Most dives are at 60 feet or less.

There are six dive operations scattered around the island. The largest is South Side Scuba with operations at Grotto Bay Hotel and the Sonesta Beach Hotel in Southampton. Blue Water Divers is at Somerset Bride in Sandys; Dive Bermuda is also in Sandys; Fantasea in Pembroke; and Nautilus Diving at the Southampton Princess.

Rates are fairly standard, averaging $45 for a single tank, $65 for two tanks in the morning and $75 for pool instruction and a wreck or reef dive.

If you want to visit Bermuda's pioneer underwater operator, Bronson Hartley is still taking people on undersea walks with his helmet dives in Flatts for $32. Son Greg has another operation in Sandys. Many places also take special snorkel trips.

Selected Dive Sites

A detailed listing of the regularly dived wrecks would quickly become tedious, so here are only a few, selected to show the variety available. However, wind plays the final role in deciding which wrecks can be dived on a particular day.

The 480-foot, triple-decked passenger liner "The Cristobal Colon" is the largest. Sunk in 1936 eight miles out, it is split in two on both sides of a reef at only 40-60 feet. The bow is mostly intact, with lots of fixtures still remaining. Twenty-five cannons of the "L'Hermanie" still lie half-buried in the sand. Though the ship has been on the bottom since 1838, it's still possible to find ornate glass bottles and brass buttons.

The English steamer "Pollockshields" sank in 1915 while ferrying munitions to World War I. Shell casings are still visible in 20-30 feet. "The Montana," a blockade runner that sank in the 1860's, retains the framework of a 25-foot paddle wheel. The bow still remains, and a resident school of 20 barracuda can always be counted on to show up. Considered the most photogenic wreck by many is the English sailing barque "North Carolina" that still stands upright in 40 feet of water. The ornamental iron framework and encrusted corals provide spectacular picture opportunities.

That's just a handful. Unless you're planning on a very extended stay, it's impossible to see them all on a single vacation. Nothing wrong with that. The diving, the beautiful islands themselves and the unusual variety of other activities are all good excuses to keep returning. Bermuda may well yet become known as an important dive destination rivaling its Caribbean sisters.

Perhaps Mark Twain said it best: "Americans on their way to heaven call at Bermuda and think they've arrived."

8

TURKS & WHAT?

Turks &... what? If you have heard of these islands, or know where they are located, then you are, indeed, a knowledgeable Caribbean island-hopper. Few people know of these islands, located at the very southern end of the Bahamas, and north of Haiti/Dominican Republic.

The two groups of islands, the Turks Islands and Caicos Islands, are comprised of 40 islands and tiny cays surrounded by a spectacular coral reef that covers 200 square miles. The Caicos group consists of Providenciales (or Provo), South Caicos, East Caicos, Grand Caicos, North Caicos and West Caicos, as well as numerous small cays. The Turks consist of Grand Turk and Salt Cay, separated from the Caicos Islands by a 22-mile wide 7,000-foot-deep channel. The islands are the least-developed of Britain's remaining possessions in the West Indies.

Grand Turk's seven square miles is the most populous island, with about 5,000 residents, and is the government and financial center. Although at one time Grand Turk was also the region's pre-eminent tourism center, resort development on Provo has left it far behind, in almost another time period. Yet that is part of the island's appeal. Many of the weathered Bermuda-style structures convey the feel of the genuine Caribbean.

While San Salvador in the Bahamas claims to have been the first to bear Columbus' footprints, Turks & Caicos present their own evidence that it was actually here he made his first stop. But there is no argument when it comes to another "first landing," one by astronaut John Glenn who made his first landfall on Grand Turk for debriefing after his historic 1962 space mission.

Club Med's Turkoise is one of the best facilities on Provo.

Travelers now journey the 575 miles from Miami by regularly scheduled flights, with Cayman Airways the most reliable. Charter flights into Provo are primarily for Club Med Turkoise guests. However, the Miami charter leaves at dawn, so you must overnight in Miami. Inter-island travel is on Turks & Caicos National Airlines.

The official language is English, and the official currency the U.S. Dollar. Credit cards are not widely accepted, even at major hotels, so it's best to bring traveler's checks.

January and February sometimes bring cold fronts that chill the air and water temperature significantly. In the summer, daytime temperatures average 88 degrees, but sometimes reach 100 on the hottest days. May and November are the wettest months.

And, there are mosquitoes in paradise. Come prepared with good mosquito repellent and most everything else you might need. Batteries, fishing gear, toiletries and other items are scarce.

Car rentals are available only on Provo and Grand Turk. In one day, or less, you can explore either island, but few visitors find the cost worthwhile. Taxis are the preferred mode of transportation.

Contact the Turks & Caicos Tourist Board at 800/441-4419. For flight information call Cayman Airways at 800/422-9626.

9

CAICOS FINNY TEMPTATIONS

Whether using 6-pound test or 130, Larry knows there are plenty of line-stretching opportunities off Turks and Caicos

Huge grouper aren't supposed to hit a plug trolled at eight knots over 1,000 feet of water, according to the captain. He had just told me that when the outrigger clip popped and the stout rod bowed. The drag sung over shouts of "wahoo," as I jumped into the fighting chair and began a contest of strength with my adversary.

The fish bulled its way into the depths as the captain nosed the 52-foot boat toward shallower water. We had been trolling a wall that dropped from 100 feet to 5,000 within a few hundred yards. The tackle was sufficient to handle the fish -- custom boat rods, Penn International reels spooled with 80 pound test line and, in time, I worked the fish near the boat.

Again, it charged for the bottom, taking out yards of line I had obtained through sweat and toil. The discussion between the captain and mate centered on predicting just how big the "wahoo" might be. They average around 50 pounds in the waters off Turks and Caicos Islands, and an 80 pounder is not unusual.

But, as I had gained back line, the spent fish finally surfaced, opened its huge mouth, and ended further predictions. Landing the giant grouper was as though hauling in a "bucket." The captain shook his head, muttering, "you never really know what the next fish is going to be in these waters." The giant yellowfin grouper later weighed 33 1/2 pounds on the Turtle Cove Marina scales. It was a new island record, besting the previous one by some four pounds.

"This is the largest ever reeled in off Provo," the captain of the Mariner III told me. "We have much larger black grouper here, some exceeding 40 pounds, as well as Nassau grouper in this size range, but you've just caught the new record yellowfin."

After the catch, my wife Lilliam and I took turns at catching several small blackfin tuna. Three barracuda in the 10 to 12-pound range and another four "empty" strikes kept us continuously busy. Two tuna on at the same time gave us line tangling thrills for a moment or two, as mate and captain scurried to resolve potential problems.

Billfish, mostly blue and white marlin, wahoo, dolphin, three or four species of tuna, mackerel, shark, kingfish and barracuda are the normal targets of the sportfishing charters. The wahoo fishing here is excellent, and that is why they had thought I had a big wahoo.

Marlin Activity

"In the winter months, whites averaging 80 pounds migrate through here," the captain told me. "It's a decent size for white marlin, but they are sneaky. They'll come up underneath a bait or lure and grab it, and then when you're on that rod trying to bait them, the next thing you realize is that they're on the other side, grabbing the lure there."

As if to prove him right, we suddenly raised a small white marlin. I again quickly jumped into the fighting chair while the mate ran to the rod. The white came up first to inspect the small bird and softhead lure on the port side, and then, lost interest. It immediately headed to the ballyhoo trailing off the starboard outrigger and took a bite. The clip released and the drag again sounded, but our panic was brief. In the confusion, the white marlin broke off.

That's how it is off Providenciales in the Turks & Caicos Islands. The fishing off Provo is laid back, until the action starts. The excitement then can be never-ending, as was our first day's trip on the Mariner III. Accessibility to a variety of great fishing opportunities right off the island is unsurpassed.

From the "Pond," as locals call Turtle Cove Marina, we were trolling artificials in the deep blue off the protective coral reef outside of Grace Bay and Club Med Turkoise in 10 minutes. While natural bait is sometimes trolled, artificials seem to produce more strikes. Most captains opt for what sounds like heavy tackle. Some

Larry's yellowfin tuna weighed 33 1/2 pounds on the Turtle Cove Marina scales. The fish was a new island record, besting the previous one by some four pounds.

fish such as wahoo and tuna weigh over 100 pounds, and if they aren't landed in a reasonable amount of time, a lot of them are lost to sharks. The tackle is sized to get the fish to the boat quickly, without wearing it out.

Also, the water off Provo is so deep, there's no way to stop a big fish from sounding to the bottom. When off the beach a mile, it's over 5,000 feet deep, according to the captains. That's where the baitfish action is usually centered. Ballyhoo and flying fish seem to be the most popular baitfish in Provo waters.

Offshore Seasonal Timing

Spring and summer are the better months for catching a blue marlin. Few exceed 300 pounds, but there are much bigger fish out there, according to local captains. The lack of fishing pressure allows the bigger ones to migrate on to Puerto Rico and the Virgin Islands undisturbed.

Most Provo captains normally offer big game fish four or five lures, depending on the wind conditions and how many anglers are on board. The natural and artificial baits are positioned on flat lines about 50 feet behind the boat and through the outriggers some 75 feet off the transom. If they're fishing for wahoo, a wire line is used to get the lure as deep as possible.

"We've had 30 hookups in one day - a combination of dolphin, tuna, and wahoo," one captain added. "We've often had four hookups at one time, especially when we go through a school of tuna. And when you have four 80-pound tuna on, it's a real problem!"

"We don't catch any small dolphin here," he pointed out. "In schools, the smallest is usually about 15 pounds, with the largest going around 40. They won't hang around long either; they're apparently on their way somewhere. All the usual techniques: chumming, leaving a fish on, -- they just don't seem to work here."

If birds are following the school, they may help locate it again. But if there are no birds around, which is generally the case, the fish are already gone. Tuna are also fast moving fish, but an angler has a good chance of catching several if the school stops to feed. Yellowfin tuna are plentiful in spring, summer and fall, and while the island record is 71 pounds, some have weighed over 100 pounds on unofficial scales.

A pinnacle reef between Provo and Little Anagua in the Bahamas can provide excellent fishing for tuna and marlin, but it's about 30 miles away. Generally that option requires an overnight trip, and if it's windy, stay home. A closer, light tackle option for 40-pound barracuda and 3 to 4-pound mutton snapper is a wrecked airplane in 10 feet of water that's located about five miles off the southwestern Provo shore.

"Mudding" The Bones

Most light tackle anglers try their hand at bonefish on the Caicos Bank stretching south of Provo. The bank, 40 miles wide by 50 miles long, is generally shallower than the Bahamas bank. Turks & Caicos is practically unknown as a bonefish destination, yet thousands of "mud manging" bones roam the numerous flats.

Lilliam and I fished them once during our stay at the beautiful Club Med Turkoise. Our guide, Barr Gardiner, gave us a little insight on what to expect on our way to the marina.

"Bonefish here are fairly easy to locate year around. They are bottom feeders, and as they forage for crabs on the bottom, they kick the mud up," he explained. "If the sun shines on the water and the wind creates just a little wave movement, you can easily spot them a couple of miles away. Bonefish are always feeding."

Summertime is considered the better bonefish season due to Provo's more stable weather.

We boarded Captain Gardiner's 17-foot Boston Whaler and, within minutes, were going out the "Leeward Going Through" Pass. We passed the geodesic dome of the Conch Farm, and headed across the Caicos Banks to an area about 8 miles from the marina.

That November morning, conditions were tough. High winds churned up the flats, which varied in depth from three to six feet. In the distance, thunderstorms seemed to be coming our way. We immediately noticed that the wind was attempting to push waves in one direction while the tide was running out in another.

Our experienced guide effortlessly spotted the "muds" where bonefish were actively feeding and stirring up further the turbid waters. We had difficulty seeing them initially. Even under those conditions, a 3 1/2 pounder sucked in the first cast of the morning. The drag sung a tune often heard on the flats as the bone seemed headed southwest toward a Bahamian island.

Five minutes and 80 feet of stripped line later, the fish was well under control. At boatside, Captain Gardiner netted the silvery streaker, and we motored back above the mud for another drift. Our small jigs were tossed into the disturbed water, but we each missed a strike as the boat again drifted quickly by the fish on the leading edge of the mud. After the quick success of our first cast,

61

we thought that catching the "average 30 bones a day " would be easy.

Shortly afterwards, Gardiner found a second mud that he estimated to contain about 1,600 bonefish. A circling gull helped to pinpoint the leading edge of the huge, 1/4-mile-long mud. Slowly we motored to the moving front and cast our bucktail jigs. We picked up another bonefish before drifting by the apparent feeding frenzy. The high winds continued to make it difficult to stay on the fish, but we located five more feeding schools and had our lines stretched by a couple of bonefish from each mud.

Best Bonefish Times/Areas

The most productive bonefish areas in the flats appeared to be those that were the most stirred up. May and November are the rainy, windy months, but the fish can be caught year round. Summertime is considered the better season due to more stable weather conditions.

The bonefish here can be sizable; the Turks & Caicos record, according to the guide, is a 14 pound specimen. Gardiner's largest was a 10 pounder, and his clients have caught nine pounders. The Provo native's guide parties have experienced some fantastic numbers also. Twice, Gardiner has netted over 120 fish between two and four pounds apiece for his parties. On one trip, his anglers landed eight bonefish over 8 pounds each!

Gardiner prefers to fish the Caicos Banks on the southern side of Provo on half-day trips because it's closer to the marina and Club Med, where most of his clients stay. It takes nearly one hour to get to the other areas off North Caicos to the east of Provo. With windy weather, though, fishing is better there because the flats are on the leeward side.

On a full day charter, the guide often chooses to wade waters 8 to 10 inches deep and searches for tailing bonefish. Most of his clients, however, are not as successful at catching the elusive bones when wading. It takes a while to learn how to sight a fish "tailing" in the shallows, and naturally it's easier at low tide.

On Provo, Gardiner's services are in demand. He is booked almost every day between January and March. There are other bonefish guides on the island, but no boats are available to rent. The bonefish flats off Provo are unlike most any others found in the Caribbean -- they're full of the battlers. Bone "barracks" are everywhere on the Caicos Banks, and you can bank on that!

10

TURKOISE DIVING

Diving A La French Appeals To Tim

Frolicking underwater with a dolphin, the clown prince of the sea, captivates every diver I know.

One of the few places to play with a wild dolphin is Providenciales in the Turks and Caicos chain. JoJo the bottlenose dolphin lives there, a free-roaming male who prefers people over his own kind.

JoJo not only enjoys people, he obviously uses us for his playthings. If he's not paid enough attention, he packs up and leaves. We humans are expected to supply all the entertainment; it's not the other way around.

Provo is also home to the Club Med Turkoise, an all-inclusive resort with an excellent scuba operation. Whenever JoJo shows up, there is one rule the Club Med divemasters insist on following: no feeding. The no feeding rule ensures that JoJo will remain a wild animal, not dependent on human handouts, and that he will come around simply because he enjoys interacting with people, not because of a conditioned response.

Chasing JoJo to touch him is also discouraged, though JoJo will often initiate contact himself. But he hasn't always been so approachable. When Turkoise opened in the mid-80s, JoJo was afraid to come close. Time, and learning to trust, have emboldened him. These days, you can look JoJo eyeball to eyeball, assuming you can get him to stay still long enough.

Because it is often difficult to photograph JoJo when there are so many divers around, scuba chief Pat O'Donovan arranged a special late afternoon photo shoot at a reef well offshore where we wouldn't be bothered by snorkelers.

To lure JoJo away, Pat subjected himself to what's known as a dolphin tow -- being towed at the end of a rope as our dive boat motored seaward. JoJo followed us but instead of concentrating on Pat, he spent most of his swim beneath the boat stern near the prop. He sometimes gets too close to them, which accounts for the numerous scars on his body. No one is quite sure why, but one theory suggests he is attracted by the peculiar sound pitch.

As soon as we arrived at the dive site, we jumped in the water to make sure the fickle JoJo wouldn't leave. Pat pulled out a large ring of keys which he began shaking. The new sound intrigued JoJo. For the rest of the dive, he bounced around us, turned somersaults, stood on his head and flapped us with his tail. All the aerobic activity of trying to keep up with him to shoot pictures wore me out.

My last glimpse of JoJo was a silhouette of him floating about 10 feet below the surface, his body arched, with the rays of the setting sun surrounding him like a halo. It was a beautiful sight, one I never saw repeated on successive dives. Incidentally, snorkelers have just as good a chance of seeing JoJo as divers, sometimes even better, because snorkelers seem to pay more attention to him.

To many people, the idea of a dive vacation at a Club Med is a bizarre if not uncomfortable concept. After all, how serious can the diving be? Club Med is best known for its party-til-you-drop philosophy.

At Club Med Turkoise, diving is taken very seriously. The highly-trained divemasters are some of the Caribbean's most professional. Furthermore, Turkoise provides (free of charge) the best state-of-the-art dive equipment. The continual flow of divers to Club Med Turkoise makes it perhaps the most popular of all the Club Meds in this hemisphere; the three dive boats leave the docks almost always filled.

In stocking its PADI five-star, full service dive shop, Turkoise selected Scubapro regulators and BCs. Masks, fins and snorkels are also provided, but divers should bring their own since these tend to be more individualized in terms of comfort. But nothing else; leave it to the Club to supply it. The dive shop even furnishes lights for the night dives.

Three boats serve divers full time, with a snorkel boat in reserve for periods of peak activity. The 46-foot "High Rider," flagship of the fleet, carries up to 33 passengers on two tank dives and 40 on one tank, with a fully loaded speed of 12 knots. The 27-foot "Santa Fe" ferries up to 27 divers for either one or two tanks. The 30-foot "Coryphene" hauls a maximum of 18 divers. The

The sound of keys intrigued JoJo, providing Tim with ample time for photos.

reserve snorkel boat, "Miss Turkoise," can accommodate up to 32. That's as many as 120 people in the water at one time.

Divers are divided into groups of six or eight with their own guide, who provides a detailed briefing. The guide also checks each person's equipment just before they step off the stern. Morning dives are one or two tanks, depending on how long it takes to reach the dive site; boats MUST be back in time for lunch. The afternoon is a single tank.

Upon return to the boat, divers find a more than ordinary snack to remove the salt taste: freshly cut pineapple (the real thing, not from a can), melon and cheese. Well, the food always has been one of the special Club Med features.

Provo has some of the best snorkeling anywhere: lots of small coral gardens with a good variety of marine life, including sharks. Most of the dive sites are along the reefs and wall that run parallel to shore, about a 10 minute run from the scuba shack. Dives are usually limited to a maximum of 80 feet. Some of the most popular sites are Two Sharks, a grooved reef system starting at 40 feet and descending to 120; the more distant Pine Cay 1 and 2, a maze of valleys and canyons and coral heads; and of course the fabled Northwest Wall, more than an hour away.

The Wall is either a superb dive or a murky wasteland depending on the visibility. Late summer, when the water warms up, tends to be one of the worst times. Northwest Wall has a gradual dropoff in several spots, but the most spectacular is the sheer drop at the Abyss. Sponge growth on the vertical wall face can be spectacular.

Divers sometimes make up as much as a fourth of the Club's 600 guests. All divers are housed in three-story, motel-style buildings closest to the dive shop, so it's just a short trek for those bringing their own equipment (few do).

Many non-divers wishing to alter their lamentable status are also housed in this section. Non-divers have two ways to improve themselves. One is to take a resort course (no charge) which enables novices to accompany a guide on a boat dive to one of the shallow reefs. In addition, completion of the resort course brings with it a special card that permits shallow dives at other Club Meds as long as divers re-enter the water within a year of qualifying. Or, it's possible to go for full certification, including open water 1 and 2. Those who come with an open water referral can also complete their final dive for certification for just $25.

Even the most hard-core diver usually finds himself taking part of a day off to enjoy some of the other Club Med Turkoise facilities. The beach in particular demands attention, and lots of it. The Club village is located at Grace Bay on Provo's best beach, which also is one of the Caribbean's most beautiful beaches. The truly spectacular strip of sand is bordered by incredibly brilliant turquoise water that gives the village its name.

Like all Club Meds, Turkoise is a summer-camp-for-adults on a slightly sophisticated level. Just about every activity imaginable-- water skiing, sailing, weight room, arts and crafts center--is offered free of charge. Club Med personnel are known as GOs (short for "gentle organizers" and pronounced "gee-ohs") and guests are called GMs ("gentle members.") Hardly anyone goes to a Club Med to vegetate. There's just too much to do, and it's impossible not to get caught up in some of the activity.

JoJo the dolphin is not Provo's only underwater attraction. Spuds the 5-foot barracuda creates quite a bit of attention, too, but in a different way. Spuds--named after the dog in the Budweiser

The clear waters off Club Med Turkoise, and the colorful marine life, make this an excellent diving and snorkeling site.

beer ads--generates a slight thrill of terror the first few times divers see him.

Spuds is not nearly as sociable as JoJo; he may show up, he may not. If he does, he normally stays in the shadows just under the boat. People react differently to Spuds' presence. Whereas with JoJo the feeling is one of delight, with Spuds it's a sense of wonder and just a little apprehension.

Spuds has a look of superiority that makes you feel as if he's done you a favor by showing up. He also emits a slightly psychopathic aura that he just might do something maniacal at any time. I thought about that a lot when I climbed up the boat ladder or stood on the rungs taking my fins off.

I tried swimming with Spuds a couple of times for photos but he was not very cooperative. He liked the shadows and I wanted him in the sunlight, so I kept chasing him from beneath the boat. There seemed to come a point when he'd had enough and he let me know it by slowing down and giving me a huge cuda yawn. Just as with JoJo, no attempt is made to domesticate Spuds by feeding him, so he's likely to retain his aloof posture.

Club Med has Provo's best beach, best food, best sports facilities and usually the most attractive men and women. Club Med likes to advertise that its facilities are so complete there is never any reason to step off the property. That's true at this village.

The rooms are adequate but, like Club Med rooms everywhere, nothing to encourage loitering. Particularly in summer with the windows all built to face toward the water--but the potentially cooling breeze is always from the opposite direction. Ceiling fans provide the main ventilation. For information on Club Med Turkoise, call toll-free 800/CLUB-MED.

The Third Turtle Inn is another popular destination for sportfishermen and divers. The facility specializes in fishing and diving programs and offers special packages. Excellent snorkeling is available off its beach. Boaters can also anchor at the full service Turtle Cove Marina. Two other conveniently located large facilities on Provo are the Ramada and the Sheraton. Other smaller hotels and villa rentals are also available..

Other Island Dives

Located southwest of Provo, West Caicos is an uninhabited island that can be visited by boats stationed in Provo. A wall runs parallel to the western shore, with the self-explanatory sites of The Gully, Elephant Ear Canyon, Rock Garden Interlude and Dolphin Dip, where it's possible to spot more than just one of the mammals.

Just a 10-minute boat ride from Grand Turk is The Wall, which prior to Club Med and the other Provo hotels, was the most-dived spot in the entire Turks & Caicos. It's still well worth seeing: 10 miles of wall containing a variety of sponges and corals. The spot known as Black Coral is one of those rare places you can still see three different types of black coral in the 40-100 foot range. The Tunnels is an opening wide enough for divers to explore; it emerges at 80 to 100 feet on the wall face thickly covered with barrel, vase, tube and elephant ear sponges. Night diving on The Wall can be unforgettable because of the eels, octopus, crabs, shrimp and the rare nocturnal orange anenome.

Yet to be fully appreciated for its superior diving, South Caicos is the place to see many of the large marine creatures so elusive elsewhere. Green, hawksbill and loggerhead turtles all can be found resting along the wall just offshore. Eagles Nest almost always offers a look at as many as 50 spotted eagle rays, an awesome sight.

A Corvair airplane sunk in 55 feet of water is home to an friendly group of fish that includes grouper and horse-eye jacks. Night diving off South Caicos is superb because of the shallow depth and the normally hidden marine creatures that venture forth at night to feed.

11

FRIENDLY WATERS

Columbus called the islands "Las Tortugas" after the large population of sea turtles, but the Carib Indians named them 'Cayman,' their word for crocodile. Today, Grand Cayman, Cayman Brac and Little Cayman are a British Colony with a population of 18,000. They are one of the safest and most enjoyable of the Caribbean islands, and the inhabitants are among the friendliest.

The Cayman Islands are easily accessible from Miami, the major U.S. gateway. Direct flights are also available from Tampa, Atlanta, New York and Houston. The national airline, Cayman Airways, offers excellent service and the most extensive schedule. It also allows divers and sportsfishermen to check their gear free of charge, in addition to their regular baggage. American Airlines and Northwest also schedule flights to Grand Cayman.

U.S. Citizens need only proof of citizenship, preferrably a passport, and a return ticket. Several rental car companies are located at the airport and at most major hotels. A driver's permit is required, and remember to drive on the left! Motor scooters are popular but certainly no way to haul your gear. For shopping, public transportation is excellent and runs frequently between the hotels and downtown George Town. Several companies also offer island tours via motorcoach.

George Town is turning into a shopping mecca with the addition of more and more shops and stores. Besides black coral (and you be the judge of whether that harms the reef), the jewelry stores specialize in a mineral known as Caymanite, found only in the Cayman Islands.

Most visitors familiar with the original Grand Cayman have slowly come to terms with the progress. The proliferation of

Water-oriented activities and outstanding sunsets are what the Cayman Islands are all about.

restaurants and malls have actually turned out to be a benefit: food choices have never been greater. However, food can be somewhat expensive - the official currency is the C.I. Dollar, equivalent to 80 cents. U.S. currency and credit cards are accepted everywhere, but change will be given in C.I. Dollars.

Most accommodations border Grand Cayman's finest beach, a beautiful strip of sand called Seven Mile Beach which is actually 5-1/2 miles long. Lots of sailboats and jet skis are available for rent. Thankfully, it is one of the few people-packed Caribbean beaches where peddlers are rare. Sunbathers are allowed to doze, readers are permitted to read, and people watchers are allowed to stare without any confrontations with bead and coral salesmen. You can also drive to the less crowded but equally fine beaches at West Bay, Cayman Kai and Rum Point.

Luxury hotels such as the Hyatt Regency Grand Cayman are well worth the money for those able to afford it. One drawback to the Hyatt is its location, across from the beach, but walk a few hundred yards and you're there. The Radisson is another good option. The five-story building is on Seven Mile Beach and many of its 314 rooms have an ocean view thanks to its U-shape. Its night club is one of Cayman's most popular entertainment spots.

Grand Cayman's condominium resorts are an excellent choice because the kitchen facilities can save considerable money. Because of their comfort, we highly recommend the Indies Suites, Lime Tree Bay and Plantation Village. The price range and types of units

Hammocks at the Tiara Beach hotel are a favorite relaxation option after a dive.

available are what you would expect to find at any good U.S. beach resort community.

Smaller motels and guest houses are among the least expensive choices, realizing at the same time that nothing in Grand Cayman is cheap. Choices include the 40-room Beach Club, the 18-room Ambassador's Inn and Irma Eldemire's Guest House. Of the dedicated dive resorts, the most famous and longest established is the Sunset House on the ironshore just south of George Town.

No matter where you stay, water-oriented activities are what the Cayman Islands are all about. The air temperature of the water-sports haven varies between 75 and 85 degrees year around, and the water temperature is seldom colder than 80 degrees. However, winter winds can make diving and offshore fishing uncomfortable or difficult on the north side of the island. The most dependable weather for fishing or diving is usually spring and summer.

If you want to see what Grand Cayman was like before all the development, try Cayman Brac, roughly 80 miles to the northeast. Some 1,100 friendly islanders live on this 12-by-2 mile long landfall. Most of it is flat and just above water level except for the east end with its 140-foot high bluff. Only five miles from Cayman Brac, Little Cayman is a narrow strip of land 11 miles long and 1 mile wide, still mostly undeveloped and with fewer than two dozen full-time residents.

As with many of the best dive locations, nature seems to have blessed the undersea region while almost ignoring the surface level. Grand Cayman is not beautiful by Caribbean island standards, but it's surrounded by an oasis of colorful, fish-laden reefs.

A couple of interesting attractions are Hell and the Turtle Farm. Hell is a small formation of jagged ironshore that some say resembles the fires of hell (although how they know for certain has not been determined). Ironshore, which looks very much like volcanic rock, is limestone estimated at 1-1/2-million years old. Hell even has its own small postoffice and souvenir stand, and people really enjoy sending home postcards stamped from Hell.

The Cayman Turtle Farm is the world's only farm for raising endangered sea turtles. The farm releases thousands of yearlings each year, but none of its products can be imported into the U.S. due to a ban on turtle products in effect since 1978. In informative self-guided tour showcases breeding ponds and hatcheries. Turtle meat is also one of the local delicacies, appearing as turtle burgers and turtle steak on menus.

For additional information and numerous pamphlets, contact the Cayman Department of Tourism, 250 Catalonia Ave., Suite 604, Coral Gables, FL 33143; Phone: 305/444-6551.

12

MILLION DOLLAR ANGLING

The Beautiful Blue Waters Make The Varied Fishing Experiences A Favorite Of Larry's

It wasn't until the mid-1980's that sport fishermen "found" the blue water action off the Cayman Islands to be reliable and exciting. The annual "Million Dollar Month International Fishing Tournament" each June placed the destination on the sport fishing map. Anglers have now taken notice of the billfishing around the British Crown Colony.

Blue and white marlin, dolphin, tuna, wahoo, barracuda, tarpon and bonefish are all present, but knowing the reefs and deep walls surrounding the islands and productive methods are paramount to doing well here. Certain techniques work in the Caymans, others do not. Although not necessary, hiring a guide to help find the most productive spots may be a good idea.

Fishing in the Caymans is difficult to top. Esthetics, ambiance and friendly islanders add to the fishing experience. Despite the fact that the Gulf Stream bypasses the islands, blue marlin and other big game species are regular catches.

Southwest of Grand Cayman lies the Ten Mile Banks with depths of only 50 feet in some places. Just off the banks, however, lie deep blue waters and some of the best billfishing in the Caribbean.

Billfishing is good along the north and south sides of Grand Cayman; one captain reported 22 marlin boated in 22 days one August. On another August day, they had two triple headers, 11 fish up, and boated five. Marlin in the Caymans spawn in August, according to local fishermen, and so they'll school then. The fish run bigger because many have roe, but marlin can be caught anytime in the Cayman Islands if you know the waters.

The strikes will be aggressive and the hookups more solid as the weather cools slightly in September. The East End depths then are hard to beat when frontal gusts approach 8 to 10 mph, a local charter captain once told me.

To catch blues in the Caymans, it is wise to watch for the Man-of-War birds that hover over schools of baitfish. Normally, when a captain finds one or more, he'll move his boat back and forth through the area and, eventually, draw a marlin strike. If the fish is reluctant to take the lure, the skipper will slowly turn the boat to slow the lure speed.

Captain Davy Ebanks who chases marlin throughout the year and recalls a big fish a few years ago that was quite memorable. When Ebanks was once working as a mate on a friend's boat, he helped an 11-year old boy land a 478-pound blue marlin off Grand Cayman.

Fishing generally improves with a change in water color. After heavy rains in September or October, the water from North Sound mangrove area bleeds into deeper waters outside of the reefs. The green-tinted water shows up clearly in the normally crystal-clear Caymanian waters. Charter captains work the edges of the stain for action.

Weather and Lure Considerations

Big game fishing activity moves closer to shore when the wind is out of the southeast. A current sweeps along the Twelve-Mile Bank at 2 1/2 knots and into the shallow reef areas bringing baitfish. A lot of blue water fish can then be caught at 50 fathoms or less. Tidal changes of only 1 1/2 feet seldom affect the angling and waves are generally minimal along the sandy beaches. A light northwest wind and seas three to four feet with a nice chop are ideal.

Lure color, always a consideration, makes a difference to most Caymanian captains. Many prefer a black/pink or blue/white combination for those waters. Medium-sized baits attract the majority of game fish here. Cut baits are attractive to the dolphin found on drifts or weedlines. Schools of dolphin weighing up to 40 pounds can be caught year round off the islands.

Five or six lines are usually trolled from the larger blue water boats at around eight knots, unless the weather is bad. The local captains often run two artificials on outriggers, one center rigger and three flat lines. A teaser is usually run on one side and a huge lure off the other. Distance from the boat is adjusted by observing how each lure is running and diving.

"They have to be making bubbles," one captain explained. "If they are on top all the time, marlin will just look at it."

When leaving the harbor for a day's fishing, the charter boats will often troll through the flats at 12 knots or so. Surprisingly to some blue water anglers unfamiliar with this technique, they have had several hookups using this ploy. Trolling speed is normally varied. When using a ballyhoo on wire line off downriggers, the boat will be slowed.

Million Dollar Marlin

Sportfisherman take notice of the Cayman Islands due to the well publicized "Million Dollar Month" tournament in June, but the blue marlin strike pretty much year round, according to local captains. During August and September, there is less competition for trolled surface baits, and less anglers offshore.

Bill Rewalt, is the father of the unique, month-long tournament that offers some giant prizes for the big catch. The "Million Dollar Month" (MDM) tag comes from the top prize in the event for anyone who catches a World Record blue marlin, one exceeding 1,282 pounds. The largest blue ever to be weighed on Grand Cayman was one documented at 584 pounds, so the chances are slim of catching one larger.

A Cayman Island record blue during the MDM will fetch $100,000, and at least one of that size has been hooked and lost each year, according to Rewalt. Other cash prizes are awarded for island records in other species, like the big yellowfin tuna caught a couple of years ago. A Springfield, Massachusetts man broke that island record and collected $10,000 for establishing the new mark. It took him about two hours to whip the 189 pound, 4 ounce yellowfin with 80 pound class tackle. The fish hit a lime and green Seawitch with ballyhoo trailer trolled off the Cayman Banks.

I have visited these islands many times and have had plenty of opportunity to see numerous blue marlin catches. During a tournament, a couple of dozen Makos were trolling the depths just off the island, and a hookup was reported almost every 40 minutes or so it seemed. The Mako group caught 22 marlin that week, with most released.

For one Mako owner, the event was lucrative. Winter Park, Florida, angler Mark Kingham walked away with $30,300 in cash prizes for a 350 pound, 12 ounce blue. I watched the "Sundance Kid" angler fight and land the fish from a nearby camera boat.

A dolphin dance is not an uncommon sight on Cayman waters.

That blue, caught early in the month, remained the heaviest marlin of MDM. It was just after the MDM tournament was developed when a Corpus Christi, Texas, angler caught a 541 pound blue off East End. The 12-foot long fish netted a 25-year old law student the top cash prize, then, of $10,000.

Blue marlin in the Caymans average 160 pounds and the whites 40 to 50. While blues are year around residents off the islands, whites hit best in the spring, with February through April considered the most productive months. More sailfish are being caught, usually taken in the same areas as the blue marlin.

Other Blue Water Action

Summertime heats up with maximum tuna action. At times, it is hard to top. During the first annual Cayman Airways Pilots Tournament some years ago, about 1200 pounds of yellowfin were weighed in over two days by 26 boats. One captain and his crew had 450 of those pounds. They easily won that tournament, which was based on total weight.

Tuna, which is a favorite forage of marlin, always plays heavily in island activity. Cayman Brac, 89 miles to the northeast, offers excellent tuna angling. July is a great month for the yellowfin, and the Cayman Bank off Grand Cayman is also a top spot to find them. The 8-pound line class world record yellowfin tuna, a 48-pounder, was caught from those waters.

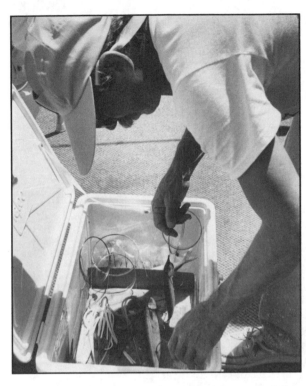

Ballyhoo is a preferred bait in Grand Cayman at certain times of the year.

Wahoo action is best during the winter, off the Cayman Bank and East End of Grand Cayman. Catches of wahoo on ballyhoo during December and January are common as close as one and one-half mile off the island.

Tides of less than two feet affect the Cayman fish less than does the moon phase, according to local captains. They believe marlin feed at night when the moon is full and bright. The best times to be on the water is the two days preceding a new moon and the two after a full moon. On a full moon phase, fish will come up and check out the baits and then may just swim away.

The best marlin area around Grand Cayman may be the Twelve-mile Bank, but billfish can be caught all around the island just four miles offshore. Roseland Bank about 90 miles east of Grand Cayman is also very productive.

Some anglers travel to fish the Pickle Banks, just north of Little Cayman, but that is a long haul from Grand Cayman; it normally takes about five hours to run the 82 miles. As a result, the productive waters are seldom fished. Most captains that do such leave the dock around midnight to get there for the daylight fishing. After lunch, they'll return to their berth.

While Grand Cayman is the more popular destination for sportfishermen, Little Cayman and Cayman Brac are slowly receiving the attention they also deserve. Boaters have the advantage of easily navigating the 80 miles from Grand Cayman to visit the two smaller islands for a try at the existing island all-tackle records: Blue Marlin (584 lbs), White Marlin (72 lbs.), Yellowfin Tuna (189 1/4 lbs.), Wahoo (84 lbs.), and Dolphin (58 lbs.).

Light Tackle Options

Plugs and cut bait tossed into mangrove areas are most effective for tarpon, which may grow to 60 pounds in these waters. The silvery fighters are found in the North Sound, Governor's Harbor, Mitchell Creek and Lime Tree Bay. Bonefish inhabit the North Sound flats of the more accessible and developed Grand Cayman and, more extensively, the Little Cayman flats.

For visiting boats, docking space is not generally a problem. Lime Tree Bay Marina is adjacent to Lime Tree condominiums, which are available for rent. Morgan's Harbor Marina at Batabano in the protected North Sound and the "Million Dollar Marina" at Governor's Harbor all offer dock space. Information on dockage and clearance is available from the Port Authority-Cayman Islands, P.O. Box 1358, Harbor Dr., Grand Cayman, BWI.

Boaters should use caution around the island's protected perimeter reefs and check in with the Port Authority on VHF Channel 16 when arriving. Navigation in the crystal clear waters is not particularly difficult. Most of the infamous wrecks occurred on Grand Cayman's East End, so boaters should take care in that area. A prevailing wind blows onto an extremely shallow and abrupt reef.

Grand Cayman enjoys a blossoming reputation as a premier sport fishing haven, and over two dozen fishing charter operations offer both half and full day trips. The sources are not unlimited, however. Reservations or advanced bookings of fishing charters are advised. Several charter options on boats ranging in length from 39 to 50 foot exist, including full and half day trips. Charter rates for up to six persons vary in the Caymans from about $500 to $800, depending on the boat. The prices include captain, mate, tackle, bait and ice.

Regardless of which island in the Caymans you fish, you'll usually find game fish eager to bite. The Cayman Islands are a angler's paradise offering productive sport fishing year round.

13

THE GRAND WALLS

Tim Rates The Wall Dives The Best Anywhere

As someone who began diving Grand Cayman in the "good old days"--back in 1978--I sometimes worry about this popular dive destination. How can the reefs survive all our visits? Are we ruining the place? Are we loving it to death?

But the changes underwater have not been nearly as radical as the resort developments topside. Whenever anyone asks me which island I think has the best diving, I still respond that for a combination of diversity, sheer spectacle, ease of diving and accessibility, nothing can match Grand Cayman.

In terms of diving diversity, Grand Cayman boasts two aspects that are virtually unequaled: marine life and wall diving. By now, what diver hasn't heard of the incredible Stingray City, a shallow 12-15 foot deep area of the protected North Sound where as many as 50 southern stingrays have almost become divers' pets. The rays are like cats, nuzzling and brushing against divers' heads, chests, backs, all over. This not only is one of the world's great underwater spectacles, it's within easy reach of snorkelers as well as divers.

In addition, you can approach even larger rays, perhaps 2 to 3 times the size of the Stingray City animals, at the 60-foot site known as the Valley of the Rays. There the rays are considerably more docile, half-burying themselves in sand and usually remaining put unless disturbed.

The Valley of the Rays is on the open reef, and not far from it is the equally amazing Tarpon Alley. Schooling tarpon can always be found in the long coral canyon, hanging in the water like plastic minnows on a child's mobile. The tarpon often start drifting away when divers try to advance closely to them, but the tarpon that leave seem only to move around the coral head and return in a continual round-robin.

Eagle rays are being more frequently sighted as dive operators explore formerly uncharted areas. One spot where the big, majestic creatures are often on display is Eagle Ray Pass, a vertical wall where they glide near the edge. Perhaps even more consistent is the Sensational Wall where a dozen or more eagle rays have been spotted.

Yet even if this underwater menagerie didn't exist, Grand Cayman would still attract as many divers because of its magnificent walls. The sponges, deep water gorgonians and variety of corals can be astounding.

Unquestionably the best diving is along the legendary North Wall, that incredible line of reef that runs for about 20 miles off the north coast. But divers need to time their visit carefully if they want to take full advantage of the North Wall, which is strongly affected by the wind. That troublesome north wind can make for impossible conditions in winter and tends to abate during summer.

Yes, dives on the North Wall are so special that the memories of each one tends to stay for a lifetime. Decades later, I recall my first look. We found a large tunnel cutting through a section of coral. The tunnel borders were thick with so many deep water gorgonians they obscured the corals behind, an interlocked network of a kind which I had never seen before but which can be so common at Cayman. The photography was incredible but brief, because this formation was at 120 feet.

But we now know of so many shallower places that wall diving no longer requires the same level of expertise. For instance, at the place called Babylon the wall begins at only 30 feet before dropping off into the abyss. It's one of the best places anywhere to see excellent formations of black coral at shallow depth. And there are still so many new places left to find; much of the wall is still virgin territory.

Because the West Wall is better protected in the lee of the island, it is dived far more often than the North Wall. Running almost parallel to shore for about 9 miles, it typically begins at about 60 feet. Visibility is often as much as 100 feet and there is little current. West Wall is only a short hop from the major hotels

Exciting deep-ocean creatures like stingrays are found at several Cayman dive sites.

along Seven Mile Beach, so this is usually everyone's initial introduction to Grand Cayman diving.

Not quite as good as the North Wall, West Wall has the same sponge and coral formations but not in the same quantity.

The 18-mile long South Wall is one of the key winter refuges when the wind comes blistering from the north. The water there is typically swimming pool calm in December and January, providing access to even more unusually good diving. The wall tends to start fairly deep, around 80 or 90 feet. What makes South Wall different is the way the reef is separated by deep valleys into gigantic formations of seemingly mountain-like proportions. If you didn't feel insignificant when you looked down into 6,000 feet of water along the walls elsewhere, you may be surprised to find these huge corals to be a humbling experience.

The East End Wall is where you often find Cayman veterans since East End diving is often the roughest and most exciting. Subject to the prevailing trade winds, the water typically is choppy and the boat rides rough. East End Wall is Cayman's smallest, only six miles in length, but its horseshoe shape juts out into the ocean for almost a complete mile. The dive sites tend to be remarkably different, even ones fairly close together, and the offshore sections often draw exciting deep-ocean creatures not found elsewhere on Cayman: manta rays, sharks, tuna and even sailfish.

As you can see, each wall section is quite distinct. It's almost as if each one way designed for divers of certain interests and varying experience levels. This is why some divers never go anywhere but Grand Cayman: their diving career begins and ends here, yet it is always expanding, always progressing according to the side of the island they choose.

In planning a Grand Cayman dive trip, keep in mind it is not absolutely necessary to make dive reservations before you leave home. You may want to wait and take a close look at the different types of dive services available. If you're a serious underwater photographer, you don't want to get linked up with a cattle car operation. On the other hand, if you're simply sightseeing underwater, you may not care how many other divers are in the water with you at the same time.

It doesn't take long to discover which charter operations are the giants of the island who work hard at booking groups of divers through their U.S.-based offices. To assure yourself a quality dive experience, you might want to select a smaller, low-key operation which emphasizes personalized dives.

Since diving is Grand Cayman's main industry, it doesn't hurt to shop around, ask questions, watch the boats leave, all to ensure that you will see exactly what you hope to and not just the daily milk run.

Cayman Brac & Little Cayman

The handful of dive resorts on Cayman Brac, the Brac Reef, Buccaneer's Inn and the Tiara Beach, all cater to divers. The Buccaneer faces an excellent reef easily reached from shore. During a typical dive, it's not uncommon to spot rays, moray eels, live conch, flounder and perhaps even turtles. There may even be a docile grouper to pet.

Most of the Brac's 50 marked dive sites are near the island's western tip where the dive resorts are located. You will find some excellent beach diving, and boat trips typically take only 5-10 minutes for most spots. Those interested in shallow water reef

It is not absolutely necessary to make dive reservations before you leave home. You may want to wait and take a close look at the different types of dive services available so that you don't get linked up with a cattle car operation.

photography will find the Brac outstanding, with lots of big fans near the surface.

As at Grand Cayman, the wall diving is superb. The South Wall dive site known as The Hobbit is as fanciful and charming as the J.R.R. Tolkien character of the same name thanks to the unusually large and odd-shaped sponges. The Anchor Site contains a 100-year old anchor with flukes seven feet across. Orange Canyon is so-named because of the huge orange elephant ear sponges, and the shallow reef called Sergeant Major is filled with the convict-striped fish.

The western tip of the North Wall has equally good diving. Some of the most popular standouts are Airport Wall and East Chute, both vertical dropoffs starting at 65 feet. In only 55 feet of water you'll find the fish attractor that once was the "Cayman Mariner," a 65-foot metal work boat deliberately sunk for divers in 1986.

Big sponges are another outstanding feature at Cemetery Wall, while grunts, snappers, scorpionfish and a host of tiny critters (arrow crabs, nudibranchs) await at Grunt Valley.

Little Cayman has what many consider to be the finest wall diving anywhere in the Caribbean. It's at Bloody Bay, where the dropoff begins at an incredibly shallow 18 feet, then drops quickly to 1,200. Every type of Caribbean coral and sponge you've ever wanted to see is at Bloody Bay, lots of them, in all colors and sizes and all in superb condition.

It was here looking over the edge into the deep abyss below that I first appreciated that remarkable color I call "deep dropoff blue," which is unlike anything found anywhere above water. It's also an incredibly elusive tint, one that no roll of my film has ever been able to adequately capture.

The top of the Bloody Bay wall typically is composed of hard corals and sponges and lots of diver-friendly fish right on the edge. The steep wall itself is characterized by small caves and ledges along what is otherwise an amazingly smooth surface. One spot known as the Mixing Bowl is a photographer's dream, with quite a few grouper, triggerfish and horse-eye jacks always ready to pose in trade for a handout.

Some would argue that the adjacent Jackson Point sites are equally magnificent, and they could be correct. Blacktip Boulevard usually offers a glimpse of an almost tame blacktip shark and several grouper. The Jackson's Reef and Wall site is large and varied enough to spend an entire vacation exploring.

Dive boats from the Brac will sometimes visit Little Cayman when the wind permits, but a problem with diving here in winter is that everyone on or off island gets weathered out of the best spots when a storm passes through.

14

MOUNTAINS AND
WATERFALLS

There's lots of good things about Jamaica. The island has 4,411 square miles of the most varied and richest landscapes comprised of mountain ranges of various rock-types, valleys, rivers, waterfalls, cliffs, caves, bays, coves and reefs. There are also some bad aspects of vacationing there, but they're easy to avoid if you plan ahead.

Northeast trade winds and mountain breezes help to maintain a pleasant climate at seaside and just offshore in the blue waters. Daytime temperature range from 40 degrees on the highest Jamaican mountains, to coastal readings between 80 and 95 degrees. Rainfall is frequent with the annual average over 80 inches.

Mo Bay, as Montego Bay is locally known, is the second largest city and tourist center of the island. Unfortunately, crime is no stranger here. If you look like a trusting tourist, you may be approached by "guides" offering their services or by someone selling drugs. Be firm when you say no, and just walk away. You must make it clear you're not interested in guides or in drugs, or your "friendly" Jamaican won't give up.

One of the best ways to avoid potential problems is to take scheduled tours to the locations you want to visit and stay in an all-inclusive resort. A popular evening entertainment option is river rafting on the Great River. The river's banks are lit with torches to mark the pathway as rafts float downriver toward a pavilion serving a Jamaican dinner and featuring folklore shows and dancing to a reggae band.

The lush foliage complements the scenic waterways around the country.

Two restored plantation houses, Rose Hall and Greenwood, are popular attractions. Rose Hall has one of Jamaica's best legends, about its second mistress named Annie Palmer who murdered three husbands and a plantation overseer. Greenwood Great House is actually a better visit for an idea of what life was like on one of the old sugar plantations. A highlight of the tour is the rare book library with copies going back as far as 1697.

Dunn's River Falls, in Ocho Rios, is the image used on many posters to advertise and symbolize Jamaica. It's a beautiful 600-foot-long waterfall which can be climbed from the beach either with the assistance of a (paid) river guide or on your own. Considering that this is cold mountain water strewn with numerous rocks and boulders, it's most comfortably climbed if you're in good shape and when the sun and temperatures are at their highest. Do take time to inspect the wood carvings displayed near the parking area; some works are outstanding.

Jamaica is served by American, BWIA, Air Jamaica and Northwest. The latter recently inaugurated a daily flight that is one of the most convenient for arrival and departure, and it also returns to Tampa, by-passing the bustle of Miami's International Customs. Air Jamaica's Shuttle flies directly from Orlando into Montego Bay, making the island even more accessible from Central

Dunn's River Falls in Ocho Rios is the most popular visitor attraction in Jamaica.

Florida departure points. A passport is the easiest documentation, but a notarized birth certificate or voter's registration card with some sort of photo ID will suffice. A driver's license alone will not.

Jamaican dollars can be purchased in the airport at a currency exchange bureau even before you go through customs. Keep the exchange slip if you intend to convert back before leaving the country.

The safest and most enjoyable accommodations are the all-inclusive resorts, and Jamaica offers a wide array to fit all budgets. It's foolish to consider any other type. Negril's best are Swept Away, The Grand Lido and The Negril Inn. In Montego Bay and Ocho Rios, the nod goes to the incredibly popular Sandals chain of all-inclusives, another quality operation. Sandals, however, has a couples-only policy so it's not for everyone. The family-oriented Boscobel Beach at Ocho Rios should please any vacationer traveling with children. And for dining, we recommend The Ruins Restaurant and Gardens in Ocho Rios. The excellent continental cruisine is served at the foot of picturesque waterfalls, providing an especially romantic ambiance.

If you want the absolute best without regard to price in Montego Bay, the Half Moon Club has been one of Jamaica's finest most exclusive properties for years. In Ocho Rios, the Jamaica Inn and The Plantation Inn are favorites of upper crust tourists who like classy service and quiet surroundings.

Villa vacations are also a good option for large families. The rate depends on the location and size of villa, and includes a maid, a cook and sometimes a butler/gardener who doubles as a security guard. You pay for all the food (including the staff) and a tip at the end of your stay is customary. Spyglass Hill Villa is perhaps the best money can buy in MoBay. For information on villa vacations, contact Sunshine Jamaica, Ltd., P.O. Box 335, Ocho Rios, Jamaica, or phone 1-800-JAMAICA.

By the way, electrical current in most places is 110/50 cycle instead of 60 cycle. Some of the older hotels still run on 220 but have converters on request.

Taxis are the cheapest and safest form of transportation. Rentals cars are incredibly expensive, averaging several hundred dollars per week plus tax and insurance; about double of anywhere else in the Caribbean. In addition, driving in Jamaica can be outright dangerous. It requires your full, close attention because of the big trucks that come barrelling around the curves and because of the narrowness of the roadways. Never drive after dark, and never stop for anyone or anything, if you can avoid it.

It is essential to be at the Mo Bay airport at least two hours ahead of departure for your return flight. When passengers for several flights arrive simultaneously, it can take almost an hour to go through immigration and security. The bottleneck is the single metal detector that people are required to pass through. Arrive too close to departure and you're apt to miss your flight. There is an airport departure tax of $80 Jamaican and be careful not to get caught by it. You cannot pay the tax in anything but local currency. If you only have $US, you will be forced to visit the bank inside the departure lounge to exchange money. If the bank is crowded, good luck on making your flight. The requirement for the departure tax to be only in Jamaican dollars is a tactic to get more hard currency out of tourists and should be changed. It leaves a bad memory and it's the last one a visitor takes with him out of Jamaica.

In spite of these drawbacks, Jamaica should be on your list of Caribbean islands to visit. Its beauty and comfortable accommodations, and, of course, the fishing and diving, are well worth it. For more information call the Jamaica Tourist Board toll free at 800/JAMAICA.

15

REGGAE MARLIN

Larry Likes The Fact That Several Blue Water Options Along The Mountainous North Coast Are Hardly Fished

The captain said he was just putting out his lines when the monster hit. He was hand-feeding the 3/4 pound bonito bait out and before he could get the line in the rigger, the battle began. The giant blue marlin towed the captain's small 20-foot, outboard-propelled boat from its position less than 1/4 mile from the beach toward offshore waters.

His half-day charter client took three hours and 10 minutes to land the prize that later measured just short of 12 feet long. When the late October extravaganza was over, they headed for the docks where the fish received much attention. It was Captain Oscar Stoddart's biggest blue marlin, weighing 486 pounds.

The Jamaican captain is after bigger ones today with a much larger and better equipped boat, the "No Problem," named after Jamaica's now-famous slogan. The 40-foot Viking Sportfisher charters out of Montego Bay. The reels aboard are Penn International SW 80's and the stout rods are custom-made. The assortment, quality and design variety of lures, teasers, birds, etc. found on the boat is all anyone would ever want or need to catch the Jamaica marlin.

The captain generally knows where the blue water action is located, having fished those waters for over 30 years, but he pretty much has the prime spots to himself. Despite the quick dropoff from Montego Bay's mountainous shoreline, few boats are seen in the waters away from the bay itself. Competition for the offshore game fish is minimal, due to the lack of a significant charter fleet in the Montego Bay area. Fuel is expensive and most Jamaicans figure they don't have to run far anyway.

You only have to go 1/4 mile offshore to catch a variety of blue water sport fish. Off "Mo Bay," one excellent area is a stretch three or four miles in either direction from the Wyndham Rose Hall Beach Hotel. For maximum action, the boat should be about two miles off the beach, where depths vary to over 100 fathoms.

The rugged tropical beauty of mountainous Jamaica and the close proximity of blue water make this unique destination of continuing interest to billfish anglers. Catch rates of marlin, wahoo, and dolphin can be impressive.

Two sportfishing meccas lie on Jamaica's north coast: Montego Bay and Ocho Rios. Sport fishermen usually overlook the pirate lore, voodoo museum exhibits, and natural scenic beauty to focus on the big game trolling. It can be productive all along the northern coast to Port Antonio, some 90 miles to the east. The Jamaica blue marlin record, in fact, was a 519-pound specimen taken during a Port Antonio marlin tournament.

There are marlin, wahoo and dolphin all along the depths off mountainous coast, but they can be hard to find. The charter boats don't always move far from either Mo Bay or Ocho Rios to chase after the bounty. They often stay within a couple of miles of their mooring because gas is expensive. That leaves most of the waters a few miles away from the docks only to the venturesome.

Montego Bay

Plenty of game fish exist in these waters. A yellowfin tuna weighing 175 pounds is the Jamaican record. It was caught on 80-pound test line. The Jamaican record for wahoo stands at 80 pounds, and the top mark off the north coast of the island for dolphin is 69 pounds. Both species roam the seas there year around, as do barracuda, kingfish and swordfish.

Marlin are in most demand by both charter clients and commercial fishermen, and fall months are considered the best. In September and October, the blues, commonly averaging between 100 and 150 pounds, migrate through the area. Most frequently caught are the smaller males, yet some giant females up to well over 500 pounds exist, almost within the shadows of the shore-bound Blue Mountain range.

Few reefs or banks exist along the north central shore to attract baitfish, so the blues normally keep on the move. When in a feeding mood, they follow tuna and jacks along the 100-fathom

Wahoo are plentiful along the depths off Jamaica's mountainous coast.

line drops. The blues are around in lesser numbers from January through March, but they can be found. Local captains prefer to chase after marlin during a full moon period.

During the winter when billfish are scattered, the dolphin can be plentiful. With cold fronts blowing through the area, an influx of sea weed and debris often accompanies the moving waters. Trolling along the floating structure and the bottom dropoffs and edges along the island's north shore will usually result in finding game fish in a biting mood.

One area that Captain Stoddard is familiar with lies westward from Montego Bay near the lighthouse at Negril. He normally gets a lot of hookups and catches plenty of big game species there. The country's northwest point deflects some of the Gulf current and causes an upwelling which attracts a tremendous number of fish. The only other boats seen there are usually from the Cayman Islands.

The Annual Montego Bay Yacht Club Blue Marlin Tournament held each September has been around for almost 30 years. It generally draws around 20 boats and 90 anglers, and contestants may boat 30 blue marlin or so.

There are not many blue water charter boats in the Montego Bay area, and the better-maintained sportfishermen are usually booked solid through the winter months. The small charter "fleet" range in length from 31 to 40 feet. There are two marina facilities available to visiting yachts in Montego Bay: the 50-year old yacht club at the west end of the bay, or On The Waterfront at the Freeport entry.

For the light tackle angler, a change of pace might be the tarpon and snook that swim in the Great River, about eight miles west of Montego Bay. The limited amount of angling done here is often done from dugout canoes. Light spinning gear, though, can be the ticket to some relaxing and fun moments in the fresh water there.

Riffles about one mile upstream from the river's confluence with the bay prevent further boat access. The waters below, though, are flowing and the banks are lined with tropical foliage, banana and coconut palm trees, and rocks. The early hours are prime time and casting the structure along the shore then can result in some snook action.

Ocho Rios

The largest marlin pass through the area, often traveling within a few hundred yards of shore, during March and April. September and October are probably the best months for huge concentrations of bluewater fish off Ocho Rios. The Jamaican blue marlin record, weighing 592 1/2 pounds, was caught off Ocho Rios in 1985. The average weight of fall-caught marlin runs around 130 pounds, while a few monsters of 500 pounds or so are occasionally landed.

One local captain has a 546 pound blue marlin to his credit. The catch was fooled by a black and red medium-size Softhead lure trolled over calm seas in the lee of the Blue Mountains. The fish came right up just a mile offshore and took the lure on its initial strike.

Several billfish tournaments are held in Ocho Rios. The Jamaica Big Game Fishing Club usually holds its event in September. A second tournament, sponsored by the Ocho Rios Angling Association, is normally held each May. The largest to be weighed in during that event was a 590-pound blue. Some of the top charter boats in these events are the Misty, Sundancer, Spritzer and Kingfisher.

Seldom do any of them have a long run to the trolling grounds off Ocho Rios. Most charters will take advantage of their prime location just off the deep haunts. Yellowfin tuna and wahoo are often more numerous than billfish.

Some of the shoals off the north coast of Jamaica attract bonito at certain times of the year.

Normally, the seas of Ocho Rios are around two to three feet. A shoal only ten foot deep exists just one-quarter mile offshore from the bay. From there on out the fishing can be productive for the blue water species. The bottom falls away sharply along the north-central coast. Depths often reach 100 fathoms in less than one mile from shore.

Coppers Rhineover is a great marlin area located about two miles offshore. The 600-foot deep site has huge scattered rocks and a deeper washed-out area that attracts mullet and flying fish, and marlin, which are there to feed. Charters work in and out of the area looking for bird action or a heavy influx of seaweed, prime spots to fish. Frigate birds can mean billfish, while gull action can reveal the presence of any marine predator below the frenzy. Most of the floating weed and debris that drifts in from Cuba or Haiti, moves westerly along the island's perimeter.

Fewer than ten charter boats, albeit the largest sport fishing fleet on the island, work the area from the marinas in Ocho Rios. Facilities with utilities, though, are scarce. The larger boats are docked at the Americana Hotel marina behind a harbor-protecting breakwater and off Mallard Beach. Some charters moor a few hundred yards further into the palm-fringed harbor in front of the Ocean Village Shopping Center. The charters normally offer half day trips with the busiest season being during the winter. Rates are seasonal and are at a low in the summer months.

16

ALL-INCLUSIVE FREE DIVES

Tim Recommends Diving For Free At All-Inclusive Resorts

Want to dive for free? Go to Jamaica--quickly.

Jamaica, the Caribbean's largest English-speaking country, has adopted diving like no other island. Dive operations seem as numerous as bottles of Jamaican-brewed Red Stripe beer, popping up almost everywhere.

This has been an amazingly rapid transformation, one that's taken place only since 1989. The last time I dived in Jamaica, dive shops were relatively few and far between. Today, diving is just another activity at the all-inclusive resorts on the island.

That's because over a dozen of the big resorts have become all-inclusives and, in Jamaica, all-inclusive are just that. One flat fee paid in advance covers rooms, meals, roundtrip airport transfers, all sports activities and bar drinks of any type and in any quantity from sunrise to sunset.

An all-inclusive vacation, Jamaica style, is hard for divers to match anywhere else. A prime example is the recently opened Swept Away resort in Negril, which has perhaps Jamaica's best diving. I stayed there shortly after it first opened, and it won me over totally; I could live there forever in one of its spacious rooms and never grow tired of the amazingly varied menu (lobster, giant prawns, veal, lasagna), its very friendly and attentive staff and the wonderful beach.

The dive shop is located right next to the open air, plantation-style dining room, so it's an easy stroll over after breakfast for a prompt 9 o'clock departure. While the first trip is out, Swept Away's accredited instructors are in the pool running the quick resort course that will have the novices aboard the 11 o'clock boat. The afternoon is usually but not always reserved for snorkeling. The Jacuzzi behind the dive shop is an excellent place to relax after coming ashore.

Swept Away also offers sailing, water skiing, weight room, workout room, separate squash and handball courts and tennis. And the setting for all the activities is a lushly landscaped ground with two-story cottages that blend with the scenery.

The cost: not as high as you might expect. The meals alone if taken in a regular hotel restaurant would come close to totaling the day rate, especially with wine and drinks. Swept Away may have a more complete sports complex than most, but the rest of its operation is fairly typical of most all-inclusives.

Negril diving has a major advantage over the other popular dive locations at Montego Bay, Runaway Bay and Ocho Rios. Because it's on lee side, its waters are the most diver friendly, so there's less chance of getting blown off the water. Mornings are usually flat lake calm for the first several hours, then stir up a bit as the island heats up (known as the land mass effect) and the fresh, cool breeze blows in from the ocean. By afternoon, it can get choppy but certainly nothing to keep a dive boat from going out.

Another Negril advantage: during the brief rainy season from May to June and September to October, Negril (as well as Montego Bay) receives less rain than Runaway Bay or Ocho Rios. That means less runoff and clearer visibility, often between 80 and 120 feet. However, during one visit in August, a heavy plankton bloom made photo efforts fairly miserable; water conditions in winter probably would be more reliable.

Unfortunately, Negril does have a major problem with its marine life. Because of the nutrients flowing into the water as a result of all the hotel development, algae has taken over much of the shallow reefs, killing off many sections. Consequently, the best sponge and coral formations are down deep, 70 feet or greater, and you have to look under ledges and overhangs to find thriving, healthy coral and sponges, the way all of Negril used to be.

Negril's best dive is probably the Throne Room, a huge cavern at 60 feet royally decorated with big colorful sponges. Care must be taken not to stir up the bottom in the narrow room. In addition, two small airplanes have also been sunk for divers.

Jamaica's landscape, with tall mountains and deep valleys, is perhaps the Caribbean's most striking, yet the most notable topographical features in Negril are not inland but along the waterfront. Foremost is the beach which ends at a great cliff formation which creates a high overlook along the rest of the

Beach diving and snorkeling are quite good in many places, especially around the Chalet Caribe Hotel in MoBay

coastline. Fronting the western-most tip of Jamaica, you'd expect Negril to witness many spectacular sunsets and it does. Rick's Cafe is the favorite overlook. The music is loud, the beer is cold.

In deciding which part of Jamaica to visit, some people may be put off by many of the current guide book descriptions of Negril as a "sybaritic, hedonistic" destination. Negril originally gained that reputation from a resort that calls itself Hedonism II. When first opened, it seemed to cater mostly to those desperately seeking romance. If they couldn't find it at home, then they would try their luck in the Caribbean. Despite efforts to picture it otherwise, the romance was sadly misrepresented. Today, Hedonism is primarily favored by horny college students.

Most of Negril's major all-inclusive resorts tend toward a more sophisticated, adult environment. Places like Swept Away and The Grand Lido appeal to more affluent vacationers.

Montego Bay, the international gateway for most divers, is about 90 minutes east of Negril. Compared to laid-back Negril which consists primarily of vacation resorts, Mo Bay is a huge sprawling metropolis. Several of its larger hotels are located in the heart of town but divers normally prefer the waterfront resorts; mostly honeymooners and those on bargain packages stay downtown.

Mo Bay currently has the country's only marine sanctuary, though there are strong hopes that it will expand to include sections of Negril and Ocho Rios. As a marine sanctuary, corals and fish are protected, which means this is one of the few places in Jamaica that reef fish are not subject to constant pressure from local spear fishermen or the reef plundering fish traps that destroy everything they catch regardless of size or commercial value. Hopefully, Montego Bay's protected status will one day be the norm, not the exception.

Beach diving is quite good in many places, especially around the Chalet Caribe Hotel, although the hotel is not highly recommended as accommodations. Ten mooring buoys have been installed to protect coral from falling anchors. The positive effects of the reef protection effort are most easily noticed at a reef where schools of sergeant majors, yellowtail snappers and Bermuda chubs willingly follow divers. Known as Hannie's Fish Feeding Station, it was declared a marine sanctuary almost a decade ago by MoBay's best independent dive operation, Poseidon Nemrod Divers.

Two other notable sites include Black Coral Alley where black coral grows in profusion inside a small coral canyon, and Basket Reef so-named for its great number of basket sponges.

Falmouth and Runaway Bay, small communities located on the road to Ocho Rios, specialize in wall diving. Most of the walls begin in just 30-40 feet of water and are located close to shore, within a half mile. They typically bottom out in the 120-130 foot range. The swim down may reveal colorful gorgonians, tube and elephant ear sponges, big trees of black coral and some nice schools of fish, such as Atlantic spadefish.

Personally, I find Ocho Rios the most striking part of Jamaica. The name, incidentally, does not derive from the Spanish term "eight rivers" but is a very bad corruption of the word "chorreras" which describes the many streams and rivers that cascade down from the limestone rocks.

Regrettably, most of the shallow, close to shore reefs around Ocho Rios took quite a battering from hurricanes over the past decade. I can remember in the late 70s how corals, anemones and sponges were thick almost everywhere. I was sickened to see the sorry state of the reefs in front of the Sandals Resort; and I was angered to see a series of fish traps containing a good variety of dying and dead tropicals positioned right next to the reefs. I saw several beautiful patches of coral as the reefs begin their comeback, but they'll never develop properly unless the life-strangling fish traps are removed.

At Ocho Rios today, it's necessary to go fairly deep, such as Devil's Reef which bottoms out at 130 feet, to find reminders of what flourished everywhere. I expect the diving prospects at Ocho

The positive effects of the reef protection effort have resulted in schools of sergeant majors, yellowtail snappers and Bermuda chubs following snorkelers and divers.

Rios will improve since La Mer, a dedicated dive resort for serious divers, is now open just east of Ocho Rios. To be successful, they will need to scour for some outstanding sites; those accustomed to Cayman are not apt to be content with the common milk run.

Port Antonio is pretty much unknown as a diving territory. Only one dive operator currently serves Port Antonio; I admit I have yet to put on a face mask here. But this is beautiful countryside and the rafting on the Rio Grande is said to be the country's best.

With Port Antonio only 133 miles east of Montego Bay and Negril only 52 miles to the west, it sounds plausible to dash from one end of the island to the next to try different sites in a single day. I can't emphasize enough: the seemingly short distances are deceptive. The winding narrow roads make for slow traffic. It is, for instance, about three hours from Negril to Ocho Rios. Almost another three to Port Antonio. You can wear yourself out driving from one end of the country to the other.

That's why most visitors stay in one area or split it only between locations for a one-week vacation. If you're going to be here two weeks, then by all means move farther along. For one week, I'd recommend Negril and Ocho Rios with the final night in Mo Bay so you can do some quick Great House sightseeing before your next day's departure.

Then, when you come back, you'll be in a better position to determine which region to concentrate on next time.

17

MEXICAN CARIBBEAN

Marketing is one activity that Mexico's Cozumel has taken advantage of for many years. Numerous fishing and diving packages are available at very reasonable prices. So, if budget is a consideration, this destination could be a good choice.

Cozumel is served by many different airlines from New York, Chicago, Denver, Miami, Dallas and Houston. Airlines serving Cozumel include American, Continental and Mexicana. Depending on their origination point, planes may stop in nearby Cancun before reaching Cozumel. If possible, try and get a return boarding pass on the trip down. Do show up at least an hour before departure to avoid standing in line if nothing else.

A passport is always the most desirable identification for foreign travel. Otherwise, a voter's ID or birth certificate will do; a driver's license will not. Although everyone happily accepts U.S. currency, different hotels and stores give different rates of exchange. Some of the exchange rates are unfairly low, so you can be taken advantage of. Best bet is to convert spending money to pesos at a bank and charge what you can on your credit card. The $10 departure tax can be paid in $US or pesos.

Upon arrival, visitors often receive handy pocket guides with restaurant and nightlife information and discounts. Another complimentary guide is called "Everything you always wanted to know about Cozumel but didn't have enough Spanish to ask!"

A flat island, Cozumel is 33 miles long and nine miles wide. Its only town, San Miguel, lies on the western coast. Restaurants and duty-free shops are plentiful around the main square. You can bargain a little with the vendors, but they are accustomed to heavy tourist traffic so they are not as flexible as other Caribbean islands.

The Stouffer Presidente's docks are excellent for snorkeling and watching the arrival of cruiseships.

Cozumel has many different levels of hotel accommodations. The Stouffer Presidente is considered the island's best hotel; it's also one of the southernmost hotels and therefore one of the closest to the reefs. One of the two fishing charter marinas is located next door. The Stouffer has perhaps the best hotel beach, a wide sandy lagoon next to the outdoor dining room, a huge thatched building. Its formal dining room is Cozumel's best, the food and service impeccable. For the most part, the Stouffer mood is very casual.

Two more moderately-priced hotels that cater to divers almost exclusively are Casa Del Mar and La Ceiba, located almost across the street from each other.

Cozumel may be Mexico's safest place to avoid Montezuma's revenge. The better hotels serve purified water and ice and wash their vegetables thoroughly in iodine. The small local eateries don't. The old rules of drinking only bottled water and only those fruits and vegetables that must be peeled first are good ones to follow. Brush your teeth with bottled water and never drink from the taps. If all precautions fail, prescription-strength Imodium is one of the most effective remedies available.

Car rentals are available, yet the vehicles' maintenance may leave something to be desired. Mopeds are also popular, but the roads are sometimes in disrepair which makes this mode of transportation very dangerous. Driving isn't difficult in Cozumel, as long as you follow the law. Traffic violators are not looked upon with favor, and tickets are frequently handed out.

There are several interesting sights on the island well worth visiting and which can be seen in one or two days. Four archaeological zones, Aguada Grande, Buena Vista, El Cedral and San Gervacio, are evidence of ancient Mayan influence. These sites are often uncrowded. Chankanaab Lagoon Park, a clear water lagoon connected to the sea by an underwater tunnel, offers snorkeling and diving, with restrictions on feeding the fish.

If anything, the beaches of Cozumel are definitely worth exploring. San Juan and San Francisco beaches are the most popular; Tanun, Santa Maria, Palancar and others are less visited but just as tropical.

Information on chartering a sportfishing boat can be obtained from Club Nautico de Cozumel, P.O. Box 341, Cozumel, Q. Roo 77600 Mexico. An excellent pocket guide to Cozumel can be obtained by writing Infotur, P.O. Box 237, Cozumel, Quintana Roo, Mexico 77600. It details hotels, tours, fishing/diving charters and restaurants.

For more information on this Mexico getaway, contact the Mexican Government Tourism Office, 405 Park Ave., Suite 1402, New York, NY 10022; Phone 212/838-2949. For hotel information, write The Cozumel Hotel Association, P.O. Box 228, Cozumel, Quintana Roo, Mexico 77600.

18

HIGH FLYING SAILS

Larry Calls The Sailfishing Action Off Cozumel The Caribbean's Best! Few Would Disagree

It was like the proverbial "Chinese fire drill". Four sails shot skyward off our stern ... and they headed in different directions.

The four sails had come up simultaneously and struck the baits near the stern, and that's when we all charged for a rod. The cockpit tossed about in the four foot seas as we attempted to back down on whichever fish appeared to be closest at the time. I, along with two other anglers, tried to find a safe niche against the gunwale to wage a battle with our respective high flyer.

Rods were being passed over and under to prevent tangles as the sails were apparently trying to circle our boat, in opposite directions.

Adding to the temporary confusion, reel drags were screaming, 20-pound test monofilament was swishing through the sea air and the mate was readying the tag stick while trying to handle the fourth rod. Breakers over the stern from the rolling seas kept us and the cockpit deck "slicked down".

All of that, and the relatively light spinning tackle, added to the formidable challenge before us -- landing the four 40 to 50-pound sails. The multiple hookup was as exciting as anything I've seen sailfishing. Four sails coming up at one time is not common anywhere, and the chances of that occurring are probably better in the waters off Mexico's Yucatan than in any other.

The first two fish up actually struck the most distant baits simultaneously and took off, and one of the mates and I had our hands full. Then, less than 10 seconds later, another one ate a ballyhoo on the closer flat line, and finally, the fourth sailfish in the group made it to the other flat line bait. Sails were jumping all over the ocean behind the "Renegade," yet it was difficult to know which belonged to whom.

Often, one sail was jumping in front of me, yet my line and fish were out the opposite direction. Finally my fish decided to head up sea, leaping though the rolling waves, just as the captain was backing downstream toward the nearest sail. There was too much activity at the moment to tag either fish. My fishing partner got his freshly-hooked sail to the stern first and the mate grabbed the leader and broke the line to release it.

The second short-line fish was also near boatside shaking its bill just under the surface, and our captain made quick work of wiring that sail. The fish had just felt the hook and was trying to spit it out before taking off. We reached the sail and released it quickly. We then tagged and released the two remaining sails without too many additional problems.

We were trolling ballyhoo across the channel from Cozumel, along an area on the Yucatan mainland side. The productive waters that day off Playa del Carmen stretched only about four miles. Each time that we hooked a fish, our Bertram was swept downcurrent, so the going was unusually slow.

Big Catch

In a 3 1/2-hour period, we had amassed an impressive catch. Our total included six sails out of the seven strikes that we had, a very good hook-up ratio anywhere. In addition to the "quad," we caught and tagged an exciting "double" which, like the others, weighed between 45 and 50 pounds.

Several other sportfishing boats with charter clients were in the same area, and most had at least one sailfish to their credit. Our action, however, was seemingly non-stop. We also caught seven dolphin of up to 45 pounds, two bonitos, one blackfin tuna and an oceanic bonito from the Mexican waters that short day.

Catching four fish at one time is as good as any boat can do with only four lines out. Even in Cozumel's "prime sailfish season" of March, April and May, that is an impressive feat. The following day, we again got into some exciting action off Playa del Carmen. Of eight sailfish strikes, we hooked and caught seven. Most were tagged and all released by the conservation-minded captain.

Catches of 10 sails in one day are not uncommon off Cozumel, and some fish can be large, up to 80 pounds. The average size sail, though, is around 50 pounds. Many of the sportfishing boats in the

Catches of 10 sails in one day are not uncommon off Cozumel. Larry shows off one of many he landed and subsequently released.

area tag their fish prior to releasing them. Comparing sailfish totals over the previous eight years seems to reveal that the sailfishing off Cozumel is only getting better. Most years could be termed 'great,' but fishing Cozumel waters does tend to spoil anglers and change their perspective.

Locating And Catching The Sails

Some of the very successful sailfishermen off Cozumel the last few years have used kites and live bait. Boats fishing with a baitfish known as Goggleyes had some pretty good days, catching 12 to 14 sails from an area off the Yucatan. The exact spot is located south of the "first cove," as the locals call it, some 10 miles from Playa del Carmen.

Further south in the Second Cove area, other local charter boats had some very good days also.

"When the water is ice-smooth calm off the island, the sail fishing can be tough," a local captain explained. "During the spring when the sails are in, it is unusual to find the waters are calm on the mainland side. Usually, there is a chop in the Second Cove area over there."

One top sportfishing charter normally fishes off Pamauel, a Yucatan village located about 12 miles south of Playa del Carmen, preferring the relatively distant waters for more seclusion. The captain and his clients are able to stay out of the crowd of sportfishing boats that often form further north. The boat usually does well there, too.

Normally, many Mexican-owned charter boats pursue sailfish in those parts with ballyhoo and plastic skirts. Spinning tackle and 20-pound test line is normally employed. The principal color that catches more fish than the others, according to local captains, is red. Yellow and green are also favorite colors to attract the Mexican sails. Sailfish don't always eat those colors or ballyhoo, however.

One of the Cozumel charter captains' often-used options when the sailfish are slow-striking is to either try to locate some dolphin or put down a "meat" line. They may use a downrigger, and try for wahoo or king mackerel. Both species frequent Cozumel waters pretty much year around.

Others try for some of the elusive marlin that sometimes are in the areas in great numbers. June and July are particularly good months for sportfishermen seeking white marlin. A charter boat named the "Boomerang" moored at Cozumel caught a tremendous catch of the billfish late one June. They landed 20 white marlin in one day.

Charters and Marinas

There are currently about two dozen boats that charter out of Cozumel. The fleet includes some that are seasonal and many based permanently in the Cozumel yacht basins. Most of the local Cozumel-based charters are moored at Caleta, a small harbor near the Stouffer Presidente hotel south of town. The majority of the American-registered boats are based at the Club Nautico Marina on the north side of Cozumel. When in Cozumel, all boats fish almost daily during the season, and are usually knowledgeable on the sails' movements in the area.

The charter boats on the island remain very busy from February through May. Daily rates vary from $100 to over $900, depending on size of boat, its gas consumption, tackle and equipment, type of fishing and whether they are registered in Mexico or elsewhere. The large yachts from the states down only for the season are not normally allowed to charter. American-run sportfishermen, however, often have invited guests who take advantage of great food and quality tackle, which some charters may not offer.

110

The small bonito that roam these waters attract sailfish to the area.

The more expensive charter boats normally do what is expected to get and keep clients coming back. They change their line out almost daily; the cheaper boats may then take what is being disposed of for their reels, according to one long-time captain. Like most places, in Cozumel you get what you pay for, and the better charters catch more than their share of sailfish.

19

DRIFT DIVING THE CURRENTS

Tim Finds You Can Go Home Again

Cozumel, located 12 miles off the Yucatan coast, has an image problem. It's a place many divers visit early in their underwater career, sometimes even taking their open water check-out dives for certification there. Then, after a couple of visits, many divers move on, never to return even though Cozumel is consistently rated as one of the world's 10 best dive sites.

I know that's what happened to me and, according to several of Cozumel's dive operators, it's an all too common pattern. The last time I visited Cozumel was 1978. I'd made two extended trips in the 70's and I figured I'd seen enough. Plus I quickly tired of the motor-sailer boat routine. Back then, you had to devote an entire day on these snail-paced craft just to get in two dives. On other islands I could dive twice and get back before lunch and take a break from the sun.

I took another look at Cozumel recently, and I was impressed with the quality of many of the new dive sites. In fact, the diving was so good, I wondered why I'd stayed away so long. I'd forgotten how clear Cozumel's water stays. After years of traveling around the Caribbean and all too often encountering either dirty water or visibility of 50 feet or less, Cozumel was a welcome change.

Cozumel's visibility underwater is never less than 100 feet and sometimes reaches as much as 250 feet. Cozumel's water clarity is unmatched anywhere else in the Caribbean, including such famed dive destinations as Grand Cayman and Bonaire.

And the incredible sponge formations--a couple were the best I've ever seen anywhere. But it's easy for dive writers to get carried away in their site descriptions, so this time I'll let an expert do the talking.

113

Marine biologist Dr. Douglas Fenner of Pacific Marine Research and the Seattle Aquarium says Cozumel's sponge growth "is some of the best in the world, if not THE best."

Dr. Fenner, who has studied Cozumel's marine environment since 1980, says the spectacular sponge development is caused by continual currents that constantly bring food to the reefs. "Elephant ear sponges, which grow as much as 10-12 feet across, are probably the biggest anywhere, and barrel sponges are very common," he says. "I have taken pictures of 150 different species of sponges in Cozumel, but on each dive I'm seeing a new species I've never seen before."

Dr. Fenner also says Cozumel excels in its underwater topography and underwater caves. Not only are the sponges and caves better than anywhere else in the world, he believes the corals equal any you'll find elsewhere in the Caribbean.

And fish are plentiful, too, more than 230 different species counted so far. Dr. Fenner says he's never seen as many queen angels anywhere else. In addition, Cozumel has its own special fish, the "splendid toadfish" which is found nowhere else. The splendid toadfish, growing between 12-16 inches long and found in holes, is among the world's fastest eaters. It can suck in another fish in just six milliseconds, faster than the blink of an eye.

Because the marine life is constantly nourished by ocean currents, all of Cozumel's diving is drift diving. Divers take advantage of the underwater winds by floating with the current, usually between one and 1-1/2 knots. Drift dives allow divers to cover as much as an eighth of a mile or more, far greater amounts of territory than they could otherwise.

Once a dive is finished, divers ascend to the surface to find their dive boat, which has been tracking the air bubbles, ready and waiting to take them aboard.

Cozumel offers an unusually varied selection of dive boats. The traditional, slow-moving motor-sailer is the preferred by those who want to savor their time on the water. These boats depart around 9 a.m., do a deep dive of a hundred feet or so, then take a shore break for lunch, volleyball and snorkeling. Following the afternoon's shallow dive, the motor-sailers return in the early afternoon.

But there are plenty of fast boats for those who are in more of a hurry. The speedier craft leave between 8 and 9 a.m., do a deep and a shallow dive, and return for lunch, allowing plenty of free time for shopping, exploring or a third dive in the afternoon. For divers who prefer small groups, Cozumel has numerous "six-packs:" small, fast boats which carry only six divers.

114

Fish are plentiful off Cozumel; more than 230 different species counted so far.

Cozumel has almost as many dive shops as it does dive boats-- more than 40, about the same as the number of dive sites. Located on almost every corner, they are as plentiful as convenience stores and fast food outlets in the States. There are far too many of them for the traffic.

Dive prices are expected to increase in Cozumel to about $50, one of the first across-the-board increases in several years. For two tanks, that's still one of the lowest prices in the Caribbean.

The one thing you don't want to do is use the cheapest dive shop, because you're apt to get service and safety considerations to match. Several years ago, Cozumel received a lot of unfavorable publicity as a dangerous dive destination. Care in selecting a dive operator isn't something you normally need to consider, but Cozumel has more dive shops than it can support. Some of them don't make much money and they cut corners to stay in business. Be sure you dive with a store that is part of Cozumel's professional diving organization, that they are a CADO/chamber member. The CADO seal should be clearly displayed in the store to make sure it is a genuine CADO member.

The best reefs are well offshore at the southern end of the island and must be reached by boat. The three-mile long Palancar Reef is one of the most famous dive spots in all the Caribbean. Riddled with tunnels and caves and ledges, the Palancar has seven different sites which vary from 35 to over 80 feet deep. Nearby Colombia Reef holds large schools of grunts and snappers, while at Punta Sur divers explore an exciting network of deep caves filled with marine life. Santa Rosa Reef is noted for its huge coral mounds as tall as small buildings. In many places, big grouper hoping to be hand-fed readily approach divers.

Since Cozumel's reefs are part of a marine sanctuary, spearing and the taking of coral and live shells are prohibited. Good buoyancy control is also stressed so divers will stay at least three feet above the corals to avoid touching the fragile reefs with their fins and other equipment.

After being away for more than 10 years, recent trips to Cozumel provided a good comparison of the types of diving available.

I was fortunate enough to stay at the Stouffer Presidente, considered the island's finest hotel. Its dock is also one of the best places for snorkeling and feeding I've encountered. Several hundred fish congregate in front of the Stouffer every morning, waiting to be thrown crumbs or sausages or anything else edible. The only catch is you have to get in the water early to enjoy the spectacle. Once the dive boats start arriving around 8 a.m., the fish disperse and the feeding is never as good the rest of the day.

Fantasia Divers, located on the Stouffer grounds, were a good outfit. The guides spoke English well and gave detailed descriptions of what we would encounter. Then it was over the side and into the current. The drift on Santa Rosa reef is typical of most of the sites. We floated above colorful coral mounds, the current too fast to stop and photograph unless you could find a wall to hide behind or a cave to duck into.

I did duck into a cave for photography, and just as I was finishing, an object seemingly the size of a miniature submarine suddenly shot through the opening. The grouper had appeared out of nowhere and at first it looked like it was going to speed straight through and out the other side. Instead, it turned and came back to me, the huge, dark apparition stopping about three feet away. My strobe flashes didn't seem to bother it but it must have been disappointed that I had no morsels to supply as payment for

Sometimes the swift current thwarts any photography attempts unless you hide behind a wall or duck into a cave.

modeling, because it gave me time for only three frames before vanishing.

On my second trip I dived with Tom Hartdegen of Dive Paradise. With all the Caribbean traveling I do, Tom considered me somewhat of a jaded diver who wouldn't easily be impressed; he was correct. I see a lot of good diving but very few things that really excite me. Well, that day Tom provided me with sensory overload, diving so spectacularly colorful that I still think about it.

Tom is one of the dive operators concerned that many divers start their career here but don't come back. He feels it's because people either aren't aware of how good diving can be or if they are, they've found it too difficult to find a dive boat to take them to the best sites. The regular milk run comes first, the exceptional diving (because it is so far away) reserved for perhaps one day a week.

To make the far reaches more accessible, Tom has instituted his Experienced Diver Program for the truly advanced diver seeking Cozumel's finest and most challenging diving. With as few as four divers and no more than six, he guarantees a special boat will go out every day. The only catch is that minimum of four: no drawback if you're traveling with friends, a potential problem if you're a couple or traveling alone. Then the only thing you can do is place your name on a list and hope others will show up.

Tom started me at Punta Sur, a spot known for huge caverns and steep drop offs. On one part of Punta Sur it's necessary to go to only 100 feet; we did another section called "the devil's throat" that took us down to 123. It is truly a phenomenal dive, a drift/swim through a series of caverns loaded with marine life even back in the darkness well away from the light.

We glided through the cavern darkness, emerging into water colored what I can only describe as deep drop off blue, the prettiest blue imaginable. Big gorgonians, one of my favorite forms of marine life, grew profusely along the drop off. Sponges, particularly orange ones, were everywhere.

It was a very good dive, but Tom felt I wasn't as impressed as he wanted me to be. "A lot of divers surface here screaming with joy," he pointed out.

Next we went to a place Tom calls Virgin Wall, a place where heavy currents are too much for average divers. After our surface interval, we jumped into the current for a real roller coaster ride. At the end of the formation, Tom dropped us behind a wall where the current wasn't nearly as strong. The angle of light striking the wall disclosed a riot of colors, sponges of many shapes and sizes including one great orange elephant ear sponge that measured between 10-12 feet across, dwarfing a diver.

This wall accomplished Tom's goal; I was damn impressed. So much so that we came back the next day and dived the wall again. I think I could dive that wall for almost a week and never run out of photo subjects. That wall is wide, and it runs deep. So far I've never been below 125 feet there.

These advanced dives are done mostly by computer. Everyone wears a computer (available for rental) so that there's plenty of redundancy in case one of them (such as yours) stops functioning.

Shallow or deep, Cozumel offers plenty of sites that should content every diver of every skill level. If it's been a while since you visited, try Cozumel again. You'll probably be happy with most of the changes. And if you've never traveled there, now is the time to start.

20

YUCATAN'S GLAMOUR

Less than two decades ago, Isla Cancun was little more than a 14-mile long strip of beautiful but deserted sand beach. Today, Cancun has been transformed into one of the world's best-known mega-resorts.

Cancun, population 125,000, is a kind of Las Vegas of the Caribbean. Major hotels' architecture resembles Mayan pyramids, Moorish castles or something futuristic. Many of the names along the hotel zone beach strip are familiar, such as Hyatt Regency, Sheraton, Stouffer Presidente, Americana and Vacation Clubs International. Cancun can be surprisingly expensive, as much as most major U.S. cities. A travel package can sometimes cut prices by half.

The Caribbean Sea borders the island on the protected north and east shores, while the Nichupte Lagoon lies to the south and west, and its where water sport enthusiasts enjoy sailing, trimarans, dinner cruises, and jet skiing.

Cancun is the gateway to the Yucatan which includes Merida, the islands of Cozumel and Isla Mujeres, and Contoy, a bird sanctuary. Ferries and daily boat excursions transport visitors between Cancun and nearby Isla Mujeres. Isla Mujeres (Isle of Women) was discovered in 1517 by Spaniards who upon landing on the island, reported seeing statues of Mayan goddesses guarding the coast. The presence of one small temple on the southernmost tip of Isla Mujeres suggests the Maya did at least visit the island.

Isla Mujeres has a more tranquil atmosphere than Cancun. Three hotels, several restaurants and inexpensive shops along quaint, picturesque streets on the northwest tip of the island are a change of pace from Cancun with its active day and nightlife.

U.S. citizens need proof of citizenship such as a passport, or a voter's registration card with a photo I.D. such as driver's license. Be sure to keep the Mexican immigation slip. Lose it and you may miss your return plane. Airport departure tax is $10.

The Mexican peso can be a bit confusing, until you get used to the numbers. A lunch check for $10,000 pesos may be only U.S. $5.00. U.S. Dollars are accepted everywhere but the value of the peso varies, so you should change them at a bank to ensure the best rate. There is a bank at the airport.

Several commercial airlines serve Cancun, including American, Continental, Northwest, United, Mexicana and AeroMexico. The latter two offer more flights from more U.S. cities. Both Mexican airlines have excellent service and food.

There are flights from Miami, Tampa, Atlanta, Philadelphia, New York, Chicago, New Orleans, Dallas, Houston and Los Angeles. You should get to the airport two hours ahead of departure, especially on weekends, when visitor traffic can get quite hectic. Charter flights can offer substantial savings over regularly scheduled airlines. The one disadvantage of charters is you cannot modify your schedule once you sign up. In the winter, it's best to go only with pre-paid, confirmed travel package tours.

Car rentals are located at the major hotels and at the airport; rates can be more expensive than at other Caribbean destinations, about $90 per day for a fairly used, small vehicle. You'll need a valid driver's license and a deposit or credit card. Keep you eye on the fuel gauge; gas stations are not easily found and roads, which are fair by U.S. standards, are not well lit after sunset.

Buses run through the hotel zone from 6 a.m. until midnight and are very cheap. You can flag them down anywhere along the road. Taxis are the choice for most tourists on the island. Cab rates are generally set and tipping is not customary.

Yes, this is Mexico. Dine only in the large hotels and never stray to roadside stands or small local restaurants. Problem foods are raw vegetables, salads and undercooked meats. And be careful where ice for your drinks comes from. Drink only bottled water, which is readily available. Just in case all else fails, bring Imodium or other similar product as a precaution.

It's almost a requirement that you take some time to take a trip back in time. Several impressive Mayan pyramids are not far from Cancun. Some of them have been uncovered and restored and others remain buried perhaps never to be found. Tulum, Coba and Chichen Itza are all within a few hours from Cancun and most are open to the public from 8 a.m. to 5 p.m. There are daily bus tours

Several impressive Mayan pyramids are not far from Cancun. Some of them have been uncovered and restored and others remain buried perhaps never to be found.

to some of the more popular sites and many smaller ruins exist near some of the hotel grounds along the island.

The ancient walled city of Tulum is only another eight miles beyond Xel-ha, or about two hours driving time from Cancun (depending on traffic). Tulum, which overlooks the Caribbean, was built by the Mayas in the 10th century. Originally known as Zama (sunrise), the Spanish were so impressed when they first sighted the city from their vessels they recorded "Seville would not have struck us larger or better."

The Maya are an interesting and unusual people. Their civilization started in Mexico as long ago as 1,500 B.C., reaching its peak between 320 and 925 A.D. The Maya built great cities of stone, extensive roadways through the jungle, developed mathematical theories far in advance of Europeans and formulated a calendar more precise than the one we use today. They also practiced human sacrifice and self-mutilation.

Tulum, which housed about 600 people, apparently was the only walled city the Maya built. Intended to help control the trade between the Yucatan and Honduras, it was abandoned about 70 years after the Spanish conquest in the mid-1500s.

The most impressive building is the combination temple and fortress called the Castle. You're allowed to climb on top of this and all of the other structures. The 13th century Maya wall paintings in the Temple of the Frescoes are particularly interesting. Although some of the work has been damaged, you can still see red painted stucco on parts of the building. At one time, the entire city was painted a bright red, which must have been a remarkable sight contrasted against the lush jungle green.

Twenty-four miles inland from Tulum is the massive Maya city of Coba, much of it still unclaimed from the jungle. With an estimated 6,500 structures dating back possibly to 600 A.D., it contains the largest pyramid in all the Yucatan, the 140-foot tall Nohoch Mull which surpasses the far better known pyramids at Chichen-Itza or Uxmal.

If you've ever wanted to climb a huge pyramid but never made it to Egypt, the Nohoch Mull is the place to make up for it. Standing at the top and viewing the five sacred lagoons with the Coba region, you can't help but be impressed by the ancient Mayas and wonder about what took place here. Across the jungle floor below, you can make out the remains of houses and small temples, almost all still overgrown.

Scientists estimate that perhaps hundreds of thousands Mayas may have lived and farmed near Coba. Today, only a small settlement remains, the wooden dwellings with thatched roofs looking very out of place here in the end of the 20th century. No one knows what happened to decimate Coba or cause the great Maya empire that stretched from Mexico's Yucatan into Guatemala to collapse and so many of the Indians to disappear. There are many theories, and it is fascinating to sit atop the great Nohoch Mull pyramid and try to decipher the answers.

A free guide book, called "Cancun Tips", is handed to all arriving passengers at the international airport. For complete travel information, contact the Mexican Government Tourism Office at 405 Park Ave., Suite 1402, New York, NY 10022; Phone 212/838-2949. For information on Club Med's scuba program at Cancun, call toll free 1-800-CLUB MED.

Because of the area's rich history, it's advisable to take a good guide book, especially for exploring the Maya ruins.

SAILFISH PYRAMIDS

The Maya Indians May Have Missed Out On The Great Action, But Larry Hasn't, And Neither Should You!

For years the portion of the Mexican Caribbean called the Yucatan has been known for its ancient Mayan pyramids. Today, the sailfish reigns in the minds of many, particularly during the months of February through July. The "capital" of that action is the master-planned city of Cancun.

The sailfish season lasts for four months or more, so those with the time and money to enjoy the action for the duration may need to get an extension on their tourist card. Most of the boats start showing up in the area in March and the best fishing is usually in April and May. Many boats catch 30 or 40 sailfish in that time period. Throw in those lost after a jump or two and the mid-afternoon lull when you have to chip away at them for an hour or two, and you're talking being pretty much hooked up all of the time.

The boats, which may accumulate up to 400 sails in an average season, will start leaving the area in June, heading for other destinations. The fleet is slim in July when the fishing begins to drop off.

The fishing for sailfish is best on a flat off Isla Mujeres, about 15 miles out. There is no sheer dropoff at the Isla Mujeres site like there is to the south opposite Cozumel. The flats area with a small ridge extends northward all the way to Isla Contoy with depths varying from about 90 to 110 feet.

It's there that you'll normally find the entire fleet of 30 to 40 sportfishing boats circled up in basically one spot, on the southern end of that flat about eight miles off Isla Contoy. Much of the baitfish found on the flat seems to be in that area, and birds are usually hovering over the bait. Often, there are so many sails along the bank that it doesn't matter where you are. You will get bites most anywhere.

Winds are usually from the southeast and the sails normally bite, unless a severe front comes through. During high winds, the fishing is still good but the boats have trouble keeping their baits in the water. You may have to go to wire line then. If the winds are around 30 knots and out of the North, a wise captain doesn't want to be out there. The wind is going against the tide then, and that creates problems in comfort.

Since you are fishing on a shallow plateau, the chances of a blue are remote. A straggler white marlin or huge sail between 70 and 80 pounds, though, is a possibility off Isla Mujeres. The Arrowsmith Bank lies 18 miles further out from the sailfish grounds, and it is there that blue marlin are caught. The waters there quickly drop from less than 100 feet to over 1600.

Some visiting boats prefer to travel to nearby Cozumel early in the sailfish season and start off there. The range of fishing is broader there; you can do bottom fishing and blue marlin fishing also. Then, sportfishermen end up at Isla Mujeres or Cancun later in the season when the sail fishing really gets going.

The Word Is Out

The fishing off Isla Mujeres has always been exceptional, and the word is spreading. Eight years ago, few people knew about the sailfish flat off that portion of the Yucatan. Today, the word is out.

There's a fleet of 40 sportfishing boats that quietly berth at docks in Cancun and Isla Mujeres. A visiting sportfisherman need only realize that lines must be kept wet to accumulate the great daily totals that many boats brag of here. By 9 a.m. during the sailfish season, about half of them are circling basically one spot.

The destination is becoming increasingly more popular, which resulted in dock expansion at Isla Mujeres. Prior to the expansion, the owner had to turn people away, and it may not be long before he has problems accommodating the interested sportfishermen once again. Since there are more places to stay and more things to do in nearby Cancun, many of the boats berthed at Isla Mujeres go to Cancun each morning to pick up their guests.

Most of the sportfishermen troll only four baits at a time off Isla Mujeres. When the bonitos come up, you don't want to catch more than four of them at one time, one experienced captain told

Live baiting is illegal in Mexico, and those trolling slowly with ballyhoo are often unjustly accused of live baiting. However, most area charters do pull ballyhoo.

me. For those boats that start early, bonitos will pose formidable foes.

When bonitos are feeding in the morning, they will often beat the sailfish to the bait. As a result, many sportfishing boats start fishing late...on purpose. Most sportfishing boats leave the docks at Cancun or Isla Mujeres at 10 a.m. They start fishing at close to 11 a.m. and fish until almost dark (somewhere around 6 p.m. during the season).

During the peak of the season, if you go for the full day, you'll get 40 sailfish bites and another 40 bites from bonito and other small fish. Bonito bites typically slow down in the afternoon. That's when the second half of the Isla Mujeres fleet arrives ... in time for the long afternoon session with primarily sails.

Non-Stop Action

Live baiting is illegal in Mexico, but those trolling slowly with ballyhoo are often unjustly accused of live baiting. Most of the fleet in the area do pull ballyhoo, but they fish sails a little different here than they would elsewhere, according to one captain that visits the area each year.

"What I've seen here is continuous fishing," he said. "You just keep trolling here. You put out lines, hook a fish, turn the boat toward it and reel it in. The boats here won't reel in their lines and concentrate on one hooked fish."

"You might hook up a couple more, or you might not, but you turn toward the hooked fish and get him off the side, not the stern," noted the captain. "You can circle the fish, and he'll be right beside the boat. You are still pulling the baits while you knock that one off."

The top boats catch around 40 sails off Isla Mujeres on good days, and the average sportfisherman may be catching 20. The catch rates do vary, though. One good boat averaged 15 catches and 25 hookups a day during the season over the past four years. That's a significant tally considering fishing at the beginning of the season may be relatively slow. During three days I was there once in late April, boats came in with catches of from 8 to 19.

Sportfishing Charters and Marinas

Marinas exist at the Hotel Casa Maya, Aqua Tours and Aqua Quin on Cancun where deep sea fishing boats can be chartered for the day or for half a day. They provide captain, mate, tackle, bait, and drinks. The Royal Yacht Club, located across from the Royal Mayan hotel, offers fishing charters. Rates vary depending on the size of the vessel. A full day aboard the average charter found at the Pelican Pier near Casa Maya, may run about $400.

Mariners and international yachtsmen can enjoy the comforts of home at the Aqua Tours marina. Any size craft can be handled in the 120 slips which are equipped with fresh water and electricity hook-ups. Security 24 hours a day and a convenience store on site are available.

Most of the boats fish La Corrientada, the open ocean northeast of Isla Mujeres, for sailfish. For that reason, several of the sportfishermen that troll those waters dock at one of the two marinas on Isla Mujeres.

Isla Mujeres is Cancun's closest neighbor and the closest land site to the sailfish grounds. The island, with a fishing heritage and natural beauty, lies about five miles north of Cancun and measures 5-1/2 miles long by one mile wide at its widest point.

Over 40 boats can be accommodated at the two docks on the island. A fuel concession, running water and power are located at the docks. The boats there have experienced surges in electricity, though, and brownouts have occurred between 7 and 9 p.m. during peak usage times.

Dolphin and other offshore species compete with the sails off Cancun.

The slips at the primary dock on the west side are narrow and large boats are advised to have their fenders out as they pull into the docks there. The new dock on the north side is fairly shallow and not for big boats with large drafts. The price of dockage is about what one would pay in the U.S. for equivalent space.

Good quality bait is easily available on the island. Locals catch ballyhoo at Isla Mujeres, so the sportfishing boats docked there don't even freeze their bait. They'll buy their bait fresh and keep it in the brine on the dock behind their boat. Then, they'll rig their baits up in the morning directly out of that brine. All they have to do each day is replenish the bait in the brine. Experienced captains in the area keep 75 baits rigged and ready each day.

Bonitos, ranging from one to 15 pounds, are often a nuisance over the sailfish grounds, but that is what attracts the sails. When a boat gets a bonito bite and stops to reel it in, the other three baits will attract sailfish as they settle to the bottom.

The area has its share of kingfish and dolphin also. Cero mackerel and jack crevale are plentiful at times too. Most of those fish are pains to the sailfishermen because they will eat whatever is being pulled behind the boat.

Isla Mujeres is becoming increasingly renown, and the area does, in fact, short-stop some boats on their way to the long-time "Sailfish Capital of the World" -- Cozumel.

22

DIVE THE CENOTES

An Excellent Destination For Novice Divers, According To Tim

Cancun is easy to get around since it basically is in the shape of a horseshoe. Most people naturally expect that all of the water activity will take place right offshore in the warm waters of the Caribbean, but not so. The protected lagoon formed by Cancun's horseshoe shape is always good for water skiing, jet skis and sailing excursions that run the lagoon's entire length and provide a good view of the entire hotel strip.

Diving generally is offered at major hotels on an ala-carte basis, costing between $35-$45 for a two tank dive, the lower price prevailing if you've brought your own gear. Dives typically leave around 10:30 and return at 3. The only hotel offering its own dive program is Club Med, which has a single tank dive departing every morning at 8:30 and returning before noon so that the entire day isn't spent on or under the water.

Quite frankly, Cancun lacks the spectacular reefs of nearby Cozumel, but Cancun's reefs sometimes boast a lot more fish. Since Cancun's waters aren't dived as much, you're likely to see a greater variety of marine life, too. For instance, as soon as we entered the water and started looking under ledges, I quickly found two lobsters that weren't at all timid.

However, the big schools of fish I encountered were reluctant to feed, probably because divers aren't present often enough with handouts. The one exception was the Caribbean's version of the piranha, the yellowtail snapper, which seems ready to take whatever you offer, wherever you are.

The best way to see the Maya ruins and snorkel along the way is rent a car.
Not only can you stop at the coves, you can also travel at your own pace.

If you're an experienced diver, avoid trips to the reefs of Bajito, Chiales and Maneliones, which are best suited for beginners. For more advanced divers, the placed called No Name is a patch reef aquarium stocked with puffers, angels, snappers, grunts and occasional nurse sharks. Other good sites include The Tunnel, Cuervones and San Miguel.

Isla Mujeres, just off the coast of Cancun, has even better diving but it is not always easy to reach since operators typically do not visit on a daily basis.

Since Cozumel is so close and the reef formations there are better, some divers might wonder why they should even consider Cancun diving. Simply because there are many, many more things to do around Cancun. Not just better shopping and better night life, but the chance to see the magnificent Maya ruins to the south.

All hotels offer organized excursions to the Maya ruins, but the best way to see them and snorkel along the way is rent a car. Not only can you stop at the cenotes and caletas (coves), more importantly, you can travel at your own pace.

Cenotes are natural limestone pits from which the ancient Mayas often took their water supply. These cool wells were considered sacred and an important part of the Maya religion.

The reefs of Bajito, Maneliones and Chiales are best suited for beginners. For more advanced divers, the placed called No Name is a patch reef aquarium stocked with angels, snappers, grunts and occasionally nurse sharks.

Heading south, the first diving & snorkeling stop is at Xcaret (pronounced es-ka-ret). It looks like only a roadside stop, but it definitely is well worth exploring not only for the chance to swim in the cenote and nearby cove but for a look at the several small temples.

The cenote at Xcaret is both spectacular and easy to reach. It is located at the base of a limestone cliff, with a large overhang protecting it.

Another picture-book ruin is at Chakalal, where a small, well preserved temple is situated right next to a lagoon; a perfect setting for diving, picnicking or swimming.

Perhaps the best coastal diving of all is in the Akumal region (clearly marked by road signs) which has a major dive operation at the Hotel-Club Akumal Caribe. You won't find the same kinds of dropoffs as at Cozumel, but otherwise the diving is quite good, superior to the immediate vicinity of Cancun. It's worth spending a night or two here to explore the hallmarks of Yucatan diving: cenotes, caverns, tunnels and caves.

Diving a cenote at Akumal can be unforgettable. Visibility may top well over a hundred feet, with the possibility of seeing stalactites and stalagmites. Cavern diving here, where you're able to spot the sunlight marking your entrance from any point underground, is within the expertise of most experienced divers provided they have a good guide.

Cave diving at Akumal, on the other hand, is a very different matter. Penetration of a true cave system requires additional training and the company of a guide also certified in these advanced techniques.

Below Akumal is Xel-ha (pronounced shell-ha), a fairly large park located 72 miles south of Cancun. The palm-lined cove provides a beautiful setting and the fish are colorful, but this place does get quite crowded on weekends. Xel-ha contains a mix of both fresh and salt water, and at the level where the two mix it looks like your mask has been fogged with vaseline. Quite remarkable. In Tulum, a beach at the base of the Castle is worth snorkeling in calm weather.

You need spend only a short period in the more remote regions of the Yucatan before you begin to feel yourself slipping through what science fiction writers call a time warp, a link with the past. After you climb your first Maya pyramid, it may be difficult to come back. Be forewarned: arriving back in Cancun can be true culture shock. The best way to handle it: go back underwater and decompress.

23

FORTRESSES AND REEFS

Tim Recommends The Diving, But Not As A Primary Activity

As experienced travelers know, luxurious resorts, pristine beaches, tropical rainforests and azure-blue seas are but some of the reasons why more Americans visit Puerto Rico than any other single Caribbean island.

Equally appealing is Puerto Rico's distinct, world-class Latin charm. The capital city of San Juan has the same colonial qualities of Buenos Aires, the shopping and dining variety of Mexico City, and the craggy, scenic shorelines of Rio de Janeiro.Furthermore, Puerto Rico, often called "The Shining Star of the Caribbean," is just a thousand miles southeast of Miami. Thanks to American Airlines' huge San Juan hub with direct or connecting service from over a hundred cities, it's easier to fly to Puerto Rico than to many parts of the U.S.

Only 110 miles long by 35 miles wide, Puerto Rico is a land of great geographical contrasts. The north coast is wetter and greener than the southern tip, where cactus are common. To the northwest, caves, sinkholes and haystack hills characterize the karst terrain. In the central mountain range, the altitude reaches an impressive 4,389 feet at Cerro la Punta.

Puerto Rico, a Commonwealth of the United States, is actually a combination Caribbean-American Island. By law the U.S. and Puerto Rican flags must always fly side by side. Spanish of course is the predominant language, but around the major resort areas many people are also fluent in English. The U.S. Dollar is the standard currency, though locals may sometimes refer to it as "pesos."

Unfortunately, like many major U.S. cities and high tourist areas, petty theft is a problem. Be protective of yourself and your valuables and beware of offers to guide you through the tourist attractions.

The crown jewel of Puerto Rico is Old San Juan, a seven-block area once completely enclosed by a city wall and guarded by one of the hemisphere's mightiest fortresses. Founded in the early 1500s as a military stronghold, Old San Juan by the 19th century had transformed into a picturesque residential and commercial district.

Today, this narrow-streeted, thriving community looks almost like a movie set with its pastel-colored buildings flanked by wrought-iron, filigree balconies. Because traffic is often heavily congested, the best way to explore Old San Juan is on foot, and the place to start is the island's main landmark, the fortress San Felipe del Morro.

Begun in 1540, the great fort rises six stories and 140-feet above the pounding sea. El Morro underwent many modifications until finally in 1783 it became the formidable structure standing today. Part of a World Heritage Site and also a National Historic Site, El Morro is administered by the U.S. National Park Service. Orientation and slide programs are offered daily.

Visible from El Morro is the San Juan Cemetery. It is flanked by a section of the massive city wall that completely surrounded Old San Juan in the 1630s. The city wall consisted of two separate 40-foot high parallel limestone block walls with the space in-between filled with sand. To discourage attackers, the exterior face was slanted, varying from 20-feet wide at the base to only 12 feet at the top. "Garitas," tiny rounded sentry posts that have become the symbol of Puerto Rico, still line the top. The wall was patrolled night and day, and every evening at sundown the six city gates were closed to completely cut off access to the city.

Puerto Rico, which has some of the lushest and most unusual terrain in the Caribbean, has been a leader in protecting its natural resources through a system of forest preserves. The most popular and most-visited is the 28,000-acre Caribbean National Rain Forest, an hour's drive from San Juan. Better known as El Yunque (named for the good Indian spirit Yuquiyu), this beautiful rainforest is deluged with over 200 inches of precipitation each year.

More than 240 different species of trees, some towering as much as 100 feet high and found nowhere else in the world, populate El Yunque. The forest is home to millions of tiny tree frogs known as coquis who sing loudest when it rains, and despite how often that occurs, each new rainfall seems to make them deliriously happy.

The relatively few tourists who dive in Puerto Rico tend to make diving only a part of their vacation, not the reason for it.

Keep in mind that temperatures are considerably lower at altitude than at sea level. It may be as much as 10-15 degrees cooler in El Yunque than Old San Juan. If it's raining and the wind is blowing, the wind chill will make the discrepancy greater. So rain gear--and in winter, yes, even a sweater--are often required.

Where To Stay And Play

El Convento, a former 17th century convent now part of the Ramada chain, is the only major hotel in the heart of Old San Juan. Traditional multi-story beachfront hotels like the Caribe Hilton, Radisson San Juan, Condado Plaza and the Hotel Condado Beach are located just a few miles farther away in the Condado and Isla Verde areas of San Juan.

Two Hyatt hotels, the Dorado Beach Hotel and its sister the Hyatt Regency Coramar Beach, dominate the luxury scene in the Dorado area just 40 minutes west of San Juan. This is a golfer's mecca. There are also 21 tennis courts, 6 gourmet restaurants, jogging and cycling playgrounds, full spa and miles of beaches.

135

Fajardo and Humacao were once sleepy coastal towns on the eastern shore. Fajardo is home to Marina Del Rey, the Caribbean's largest marina which opened in 1989, and plans are underway for new resort expansion. Humacao offers the sprawling and ever-expanding Mediterranean-styled Palmas del Mar resort consisting of five villages, private harbor, marina and golf course.

In touring the countryside, the best places to stay are the Paradores, a chain of 17 inns located in some of the most historic and scenic places. Although they do have swimming pools, the Paradores are simpler and much less expensive than the big resorts.

Old San Juan is not just an historic shell but a thriving, very lively place, particularly at night when the big department stores close down and the small cafes come to life.

As cruise ship enthusiasts are well aware, Old San Juan is a shopper's paradise for jewelry, art works, leather goods and souvenir items. A good selection of designer clothes and shoes are also available in the Condado and Isla Verde areas.

The Caribbean's largest shopping mall, the Plazas Las Americas, is located in San Juan's business district, Hato Rey. The mall is more than three miles long with 192 shops. Not only may prices be as much as 30-40 percent lower than stateside, there is the added bonus of no sales tax. And, of course, rum is made in Puerto Rico, so that is always a good buy.

But What About The Diving?

Although Puerto Rico attracts many American tourists, it is not a major dive destination, and there are several reasons for this.

On some islands, such as Grand Cayman, divers were responsible for starting tourism in the first place. On the other hand, Puerto Rico became an important tourist destination long before diving was popular. With so many people visiting on cruise ships, staying in the hotels, playing golf and gambling at the casinos, divers really aren't that important to the Puerto Rican economy, and little has been done to lure divers there.

Furthermore, Puerto Rican waters don't have the same quality reputation for visibility and marine life that the neighboring U.S. and British Virgin islands do. Most divers aren't willing to spend their vacation money in untested waters (unless they've been everywhere else) so the standoff has become mutual. The relatively few tourists who dive in Puerto Rico tend to make diving only a part of their vacation, not the reason for it.

But if you do want to get wet, where should you go?

San Juan has two reef systems, known as the Inside Reef and the Outer Reef. The Inside formation, enclosed by a barrier, has many shallow sections and lots of tropical fish. The Outer Reef offers the better diving, down deep, with several caves and caverns.

The San Juan setting is appropriate for casual marine swimmers, but the better diving is away from the well developed metropolis.

The east coast city of Fajardo is Puerto Rico's boating capital. Besides shallow water snorkeling in close, it's possible to visit several islands just offshore: Diablo Island usually has good visibility year-round and an interesting dropoff starting at 65 feet, while Palomino Island offers shallower sites.

Humacao is another growing east coast resort community that has a log of at least 20 different dive sites. One of its better spots is the mini-wall at Basslet Reef, which can be excellent for photos. Caves, tunnels and overhangs shelter tropicals as well as lobster and turtles. A sightseeing swim known as The Drift takes place at 60 feet past large coral heads; visibility may extend as much as 80 to 100 feet.

The sleepy fishing village of La Parguera has an amazing vertical wall for more than 20 miles along the south coast that comes within four miles of land at some points. Trees of black coral, deepwater gorgonians and bright sponges cover sections of the wall which starts at 45 feet, slopes to 90 and then plummets thousands of feet into the Puerto Rico Trench. The area around Aguadilla is known for its sandy bottom and close-to-shore dropoff. The Crash Boat site long has been popular with locals.

The archipelago of Culebra boasts some of Puerto Rico's best diving, offering everything from coral reef systems to caves, caverns, wrecks and walls with colorful topical fish providing a constant panoramic background. Fans grow as much as four to five feet across and corals are typically healthy. Grunts, angelfish and jacks are just a few of the many different fish varieties. An excellent spot for photography, though current may be encountered in some sections.

Isabela, on Puerto Rico's northern coast, offers a good deal of shore diving. It's just a short swim out from the beach to some impressive coral caves and caverns, some large enough to drive a bus through.

The number of dive operators is small compared to other water sports activities, but keep in mind that all dive boats are licensed by the U.S. Coast Guard and carry radios. You won't have to deal with some of the questionable tubs that pass for dive boats on other islands.

For additional information, contact the Puerto Rico Tourism Office, 575 Fifth Ave., New York, NY 10017; toll-free nationwide at 800/223-6530 or in New York state at 212/599-6262.

24

LATIN BILLFISH

While Billfish Tournaments Are Common, These Productive Waters Are Under-fished, According To Larry

Situated in the northern Caribbean, Puerto Rico offers a blend of American and Spanish Culture and some of the best fishing around. While many go to the island for the white beaches and five-star accommodations, others know of the blue water fishing commonly found off the north shore within sight of land. The closeness of the action is the advantage that the island has over many other sport fishing destinations.

The well-known Puerto Rico Trench is the deepest hole in the Atlantic Ocean and second in depth only to the Mariana Trench in the Western Pacific Ocean. Just north of the island, the "Milwaukee Deep" ocean floor at 28,374 feet is reputedly the deepest spot in the Atlantic. The well-known stretch of ocean canyon off Puerto Rico that plunges to more than six miles starts just 4 or 5 miles out of San Juan harbor.

Most boats start fishing as soon as they clear the harbor entrance and the historic fortress, El Morro. The fort, built in the 1500s, has towered over the entrance to San Juan Bay for centuries and is an interesting landmark.

The Trench serves as a major migratory route for blue marlin and other pelagic species; that's why some call it "blue marlin alley." The big game fish move eastward by the 600-mile long island searching for their preferred water temperature and an abundant food supply.

Along the edge of the Trench is an upwelling of nutrients, creating a birthing ground for the food chain. With such fertility, sport fish are abundant. The island once held the all-tackle world record for blue marlin, and the big ones are still there, along with other big game fish such as white marlin, sailfish, yellowfin and bluefin tuna, wahoo and dolphin.

Blue marlin congregate in greatest numbers between May and October, and you can usually count on a couple of marlin strikes per day on a productive day during the peak season. Occasionally, several more strikes and catches are recorded, but that's certainly not the norm. Neither is a 700 or 800 pound fish.

Giants are taken once in awhile, however. The biggest blue taken off the island was just shy of the 1,000 pound mark, yet most captains claim to have had on even larger fish. Some believe it is just a matter of time before Puerto Rico, just 80 miles west of St. Thomas, reclaims the world record for blue marlin.

Blue Water Variety

While the biggest blues inhabit the trench primarily in the summer, the action on smaller blues and most of the other species occurs year around. As the air and water cool, the catches of blues become fewer in number and smaller fish are the norm. For example, they may average around 100 pounds in October and November. In December and January, there are primarily just a few baby blues taken.

White marlin swim these water almost year around, but they are most abundant from January through May when the blues have basically taken a sabbatical. Sailfish and wahoo are frequent catches in the fall months, when the charter boat's heavyweight tackle often switches from primarily 80s to 50s or 30s. Wahoo are often caught off the southeast coast of Puerto Rico around a sea mount. Wahoo in excess of 100 pounds are reportedly caught off Humacao.

In the cooler months, tuna may lurk under massive schools of bonito or dolphin. November through March is the peak period to catch a big dolphin. They will range from about 10 pounds up to 65, and January is one month many of the charters will bring in 15 or 20 of the good eating fish each day. On some days, the numbers and catches can get wild!

Since bonito and dolphin run in the winter months, the tuna fishing for yellowfin and blackfin is best then. Feathers, squid rigs and softhead bubblers all produce tuna action in the new year. Finding schools of flying fish often keys in the charter captains to productive stretches. So does the bird traffic overhead.

The biggest blues migrate through the Puerto Rico Trench primarily in the summer, yet action on smaller blues occurs year around.

Chartering Choices

The proximity of the fishing off the north coast provides half-day charters with a good chance at success on marlin or other game fish high on the demand list. Since the coast has no gradual sloping shelf, underwater mountains or reefs, the fish can be almost anywhere. As a result, the charter boats have little in the way of structure that merits special attention; they often simply troll over a wide area.

Some natural bait enthusiasts use mackerel, mullet or bonefish for marlin and rely on ballyhoo for dolphin, sailfish and wahoo. Usually, though, the charter boats prefer to troll artificial lures, since they have to cover a lot of ground sometimes. That doesn't mean they won't have a large bait rigged on heavy tackle standing by for a potential trophy that may swim through the lure spread.

Because of the possibility of hooking a giant and the great depths just off the coast, heavy gear is emphasized. Plenty of heavy line capacity, precise drag adjustments and function and expert boat control are vital to landing one of the big marlin that swim in the Trench. The Puerto Rico monsters have often emptied reels not up to the task.

Most visiting sportfishermen charter boats from the San Juan or Humacao harbors. Most boats range from 30 to 55 feet in length and are priced according to equipment, trip length and size (and luxury) of craft. The crews are experienced and safety conscious. Captains are licensed and their insured boats have been inspected by the U.S. Coast Guard.

The charter boats provide everything you'll need to fish. They will normally carry 4 to 6 passengers. Rates vary from around $300 for a half day trip to $550 for a full day on an average charter out of San Juan. Arrangements can be made through most of the major hotels, resorts and marinas.

For those traveling yachtsmen looking for a berth, the popular Club Nautico de San Juan in the heart of the Condado district is convenient to business and entertainment in the heart of San Juan. The Marina Puerto Del Rey is a giant full-service marina about 30 miles east of San Juan. It is very popular with cruisers and traveling sportfishermen.

Tournament and Visit Scheduling

Home of perhaps the most popular tournament in the Caribbean, the International Billfish Tournament (normally held out of Puerto Rico's Club Nautico) draws about 100 boats and 300 anglers each year. The event is almost 40 years old and has a battery of corporate sponsors. The prize structure attracts the crowds, which catch well over 100 blues in just four days of fishing. In 1988, they caught and released 190 marlin in this event. For further information, contact the Club Nautico de San Juan at P.O. Box 1133, San Juan, Puerto Rico, 00902 or phone (809) 722-0177.

San Juan, on the north coast of the island, is home to several other billfish tournaments each year. So are the towns of Rincon, Mayaguez and Boqueron on the west coast and Fajardo at the eastern end of the Island of Ponce. In fact, Puerto Rico's sport fishermen are enthusiastic about such activities. Despite that, the waters off Puerto Rico are not over-fished. Add to that the fact that Puerto Rico has been a leader in billfish conservation in recent years, and you have to note a bright future for the area.

If you want to plan a big marlin trip, set your schedule for a full moon period which is usually prime for the giants. The big boys that migrate down the north coasts of Cuba, Haiti and the Dominican

Republic seem to feed heavily around the full moon. Locals reason that it is because there is more baitfish activity on the surface then.

The trade winds off the island usually average between 10 and 15 knots during the summer, which builds the seas to a fair chop. In the winter, things can get worse. Frontal winds from the north can make the seas off San Juan very rough.

There is some overlooked tarpon fishing in the bays off the southwest coast of the island. Boqueron Bay offers tarpon and an occasional snook in the mangroves. Some small boats charter for light tackle tarpon fishing in low light (dusk and dawn times) on the lagoons around San Juan. Bonefish in some of the flats area are sometimes a target of inshore fishermen.

Snappers also abound in Puerto Rico, and many of them are caught at night about one half mile offshore in the bay. Most of the action on this island, however, will evolve around the blue marlin. Most everyone is trying to catch a big one here, one that will set the next world record.

25

AMERICA'S PLAYGROUND

The U.S. Virgin Islands is an ideal 'foreign' destination for those making their first trip out of the country. It's far enough to provide a Caribbean adventure, yet it is very much a part of the U.S.

American Airlines has direct flights from many U.S. cities to St. Thomas; St. John does not have an airport. Delta flies to San Juan where you can connect with the other major carriers. We recommend flying one of the major carriers into St. Thomas or St. Croix directly, avoiding San Juan. If that is not possible, fly only American Airlines if you expect reliable service from San Juan.

At least, you face no long immigration lines to further test your patience and endurance. However, you still need some proof of citizenship to enter. And you'll need to clear customs upon departure. When several flights are departing at the same time, customs can get very backed up.

Located 1,500 miles southeast of New York and 1,100 miles southeast of Miami, the USVI were discovered by Columbus on his second voyage in 1493. For most of their history, the islands were owned by Denmark, until the U.S. purchased them for $25 million in gold in 1917 to help protect the Panama Canal during WWI.

Although St. Croix is the largest of the group, St. Thomas is the capital and by far the most developed and visited. It's also the "crime capital of the Caribbean" and this is a well kept secret by the area tourist industry.

Charlotte Amalie's fantasy-looking harbor (white and pastel houses are bright beacons against the rich green hills) is the No. 1 cruise port in the entire Caribbean. It's no wonder then that shopping is probably the most popular land attraction in what is probably the Caribbean's best duty free area. As an added enticement, customs regulations now allow you to take back $1,200 worth of merchandise duty free.

St. Thomas is an island of contrasts. The harbor area is like any large American city with its traffic and hustle and bustle and petty theft. But up in the hills a more tranquil pace prevails. You can even find cattle grazing in emerald fields in a countryside that reminds many travelers of France. St. Thomas also has eight outstanding beaches; heart-shaped Magens Bay was named as one of the world's 10 most beautiful beaches by "National Geographic" magazine.

The USVI have more hotels per square inch of land space than anywhere else in the Caribbean. Some of the better resorts on St. Thomas are Frenchman's Reef, Sapphire Beach Resort, Point Pleasant Resort and the Stouffer Grand Beach. For something smaller, try Blackbeard's Castle, a small 16-room inn on a hill overlooking Charlotte Amalie; but it is well away from beaches, marinas and dive operators.

One of the interesting island attractions is Coral World. The three-level dome tower is an underwater observatory and marine park providing a look at the real ocean outside. Another level is filled mostly with aquarium tanks for a close-up look of colorful fish and other creatures.

Taxis and rental cars are available everywhere. In exploring St. Thomas, it's a good idea not to wander off the beaten track very far and to take a taxi tour first to get a feel for the island. Road signs are almost nonexistent and traveling on your own can get confusing. Even though you're in the U.S. Virgin Islands, all driving is on the left. It's a carry over from the Danish days.

By the way, swimsuits and bikinis are fine for the beach but are prohibited in downtown Charlotte Amalie. They're also frowned on in St. Croix.

St. John

Just a 20-minute ferry ride from St. Thomas is St. John, an island almost the size of St. Thomas but without any of its big city ways. Most of St. John is a national park, and consequently most of the waters surrounding it are well protected. Cruz Bay, the main town, is a tiny backwater village compared to thriving Charlotte Amalie, but for those who like to feel they're in the uncrowded Caribbean, St. John is the place to be.

St. John is well worth a visit for the island views. You'll find several more excellent beaches, particularly at Maho Bay, and some interesting old sugar mill ruins at the Annaberg Plantation

Cinnamon Bay on St. John is one of the most scenic areas in the U.S.V.I.

built in the 1780s. The National Park Service, in charge of most of the island, conducts guided shore walks on the shallow flats in front of the plantation every Monday afternoon at 2 p.m. Simply show up to join the outing.

Places to stay include the beautiful Hyatt Regency Virgin Grand. The highly touted Caneel Bay Resort is pretty shaggy looking these days; further, it lacks air conditioning. The grounds are far more impressive than the rooms.

St. John is quite easy to explore, and a rental car is the best way to move around the island. The taxi fares would eat you alive.

St. Croix

The largest of the U.S. Virgins, St. Croix covers a total of 82.2 square miles (compared to St. Thomas' 28 square miles and St. John's 20 square miles.) It is separated into two distinct regions marked by the cities of Christiansted and Frederiksted.

The Danish influence is still quite pronounced, particularly at Fort Christiansvaern painted a bright yellow, a color the Danes seemed to enjoy. Begun in 1738, it was partially destroyed by a hurricane and then rebuilt in 1837. The fort is restored to its 1830s period and contains an exhibit on local military history.

The nearby Steeple Building was built as a Lutheran Church by the Danes in 1735. Now restored, it is a National Park Museum with archaeological, black history and architectural exhibits. The Government House is considered one of the finest examples of Danish architecture remaining in the islands, originally a home for a Danish merchant (obviously a very wealthy one) in 1747.

At the western-most tip of St. Croix is Frederiksted, founded in 1751. Since its inception it has been St. Croix's main deepwater harbor and even today all cruise ships still dock here, then transport visitors to Christiansted and elsewhere by bus. The town's most prominent feature is Fort Frederik, site of the emancipation of slaves in 1848; for this reason, the town today is still sometimes called "Freedom City" by locals.

The finest surviving sugar plantation museum is the Whim Estate just west of Frederiksted. The oval-shaped, high ceiling great house has been carefully restored and is furnished with period antiques throughout. Besides the cookhouse, the Whim Estate has the island's most photogenic windmill, complete with giant white blades.

Accommodations on St. Croix include the Buccaneer Hotel just east of Christiansted and the Carambola Beach Resort and Golf Club on Davis Bay, generally considered the best. Carambola is for those seeking total seclusion since it is about 30 minutes from Christiansted. The hotel shuttle runs several times daily; a taxi ride is $20 one-way. In Christiansted situated right on the waterfront or just a few steps away are the Caravalle Hotel, Anchor Inn, Club Comanche and King's Alley.

For travel information, contact the U.S. Virgin Islands Division of Tourism, 2655 Le Jeune Rd #907, Coral Gables, FL 33134 or call 305/442-7200.

26

RECORD MARLIN CAPITAL

Larry Is Convinced That The Famous North Drop Provides The Most Consistent Big Marlin Action In Caribbean/ Atlantic Waters

The most popular sportfishing area in all of the Virgin Islands lies about 20 miles northeast of St. Thomas and 17 miles north of the mountainous BVI island of Jost Van Dyke. The areas there, called "Saddle," "Breast," "Pregnant Lady" and "Gun Sight," are famous for producing giant blue marlin. The latter three names are landmarks on St. Thomas and St. John that the sportfishermen use to locate the hotspots along the famous North Drop area.

The "100 fathom dropoff," as the North Drop is called, swoops down from the top of a shelf at about 30 fathoms to about 140 fathoms before tapering off to a gradual descent down to 600 fathoms, then plunging on into the Puerto Rico Trench. The Trench is reportedly the deepest hole in the Atlantic Ocean. The North Drop ultimately falls to more than six miles there.

One of the world's deepest canyons, the Trench is a natural roadway for some of the biggest fish to navigate around peaks rising above the surface. The migratory path for pelagic species such as marlin allows them to locate the preferred temperature range and food supply they require.

The Trench hits the Saddle, or "Corner" as it is also known, causing an upwelling of nutrients, a rich food source for phytoplankton. In turn, zooplankton are attracted, then baitfish

149

and the rest of the food chain. With such fertility, the sport fish are abundant. The Saddle also causes the current to turn in a large eddy that helps to suspend the plankton-rich water and, as some speculate, the marlin's fertilized eggs. Whether blue marlin spawn here or not is still apparently conjecture.

The North Drop is often alive with yellowfin tuna, dolphin, wahoo and white marlin, and it is very possible to get a grand slam of a blue, white and sailfish here. White marlin and tuna are most common during the spring and fall, while the best month for sails is December. Most of the focus is on some of the biggest blues in the Caribbean and Atlantic, however. In fact, many blue water world records have been set here. The tuna-fed marlin tend to be longer and heavier there than those at other Caribbean locations.

The still-standing all-tackle blue marlin record of 1,282 pounds was caught off the North Drop in 1977, as well as many of the other world records caught in the Virgin Islands. In fact, since 1963, a dozen blue marlin world records and another dozen other world records have been set in the waters north of Red Hook, St. Thomas. Not all of the marks are held by professionals, either. A six-year old boy holds one world record and a woman's first blue marlin is another. Another blue of 1,190 pounds was taken in 1986.

The marlin population in the nearby waters bordering the Puerto Rico Trench is much larger. Most of the area's giants over 800 pounds have been caught by charters from St. Thomas in the U.S.V.I. off the North Drop, Up to 9 marlin in one day has been caught by an angler here.

Giant's Quarters

Several wahoo records have also come from the North Drop. The wahoo are caught year around, but the best time is from September to May. Large specimens of cobia, king mackerel, bonito, dolphin, blackfin tuna and other pelagic species are often side by side with the more popular sport fish swimming these waters. Dolphin are caught in most months except the very hottest, but spring is the best time to tangle with several. The best month to catch a cobia is January.

The boat ride from many of the resorts to the North Drop is 20 miles or so, around an hour or more on most vessels, but the marlin population is worth the time expense. St. John and St. Thomas, both in the U.S.V.I. and Tortola in the B.V.I., are all about the same distance away from that action.

Red Bailey, of St. Thomas, has been captain of the "Abigale III" for 17 years and is very familiar with the North Drop area. The largest blue marlin taken aboard his boat in that area weighed 710

The North Drop is often alive with yellowfin tuna, dolphin, wahoo and marlin.

pounds, and a number of his clients have caught records, including the existing 12 pound test line world record, a 448 pound blue marlin caught in 1972.

Not coincidentally, the daughter of the record-holder returned in 1988 to fish with Bailey at the North Drop and hooked a blue on 12 pound line that was estimated to be over 500 pounds. The leader wire popped in the mate's hand as he tried to land the fish.

Marlin Mecca Attraction

"There's a body of fish coming out of the Caribbean and going to the North Drop," explained one captain, "and they get pounded hard by the St. Thomas boats every day. Maybe 25 boats hit a three-mile stretch along the drop every day. The North Drop is where you can see more birds and tunas than anywhere else in the Caribbean."

151

Charter captains encourage anglers to tag and release their marlin. In fact, a strong tagging ethic has evolved here over the past five years.

The North Drop is so fertile that it attracts a variety of game fish and tiger, hammerhead and bull sharks. The latter threesome will attack hooked fish at times. The sport fish here are usually wild, though. The water temperature may make a difference in the activity of the fish. It is almost two degrees cooler than other areas south of this marlin mecca. Flying fish, though, may be more abundant in many other waters.

The fishing off the North Drop was discovered many years ago by two daring souls. Until then, the visiting sportfishing boats would fish off Puerto Rico because it was so well known. No one wanted to break the mold. But two guys decided to take a chance and boat out to the North Drop and check it out.

Today, there are many tournaments held out of St. Thomas. They generally offer about a 1.5 to 2.0 blue marlin per boat catch rate over four days. The annual International Open Blue Marlin ("Boy Scout") Tournament held in the U.S.V.I. usually finds at least 50 boats fishing over the North Drop. The area attracts marlin boats from the British Virgin Island ports, as well as from St. Thomas.

One of the best tournaments ever occurred in 1987 at the St. Thomas Boy Scout Tournament. Eleven blue marlin were caught in two days off the North Drop by one boat. Over 100 marlin were caught by 23 boats that year, including one weighing 529 pounds.

Charter Services

Most of the tournaments and charter boats that work the North Drop are based in the Red Hook Harbor near the eastern tip of St. Thomas. There are several marinas offering well-equipped boats for hire; St. Thomas Sportfishing Center, American Yacht Harbor and Fish Hawk Marina are three. Another 6 to 8 marinas offer some charter services and slips for visiting boats also. Most of the charter captains and visiting sportfishing boats use 30- and 50-pound tackle and troll both natural baits and artificials simultaneously for blue marlin that average around 300 pounds.

The charter captains in Red Hook encourage anglers to tag and release their marlin. In fact, a strong tagging ethic has evolved here over the past five years. Almost 80 to 90 percent of the blues caught are tagged, according to reports.

Charters are also available on St. John and St. Croix, the southern-most island in the chain. Good fishing grounds off the later can be found at Lang Bank where wahoo, kingfish and dolphin are taken. Tournaments are also held at St. Croix in the spring and fall. Fishing interest of serious big game chasers off St. Croix, however, is not as peaked as it is on the other islands. The marlin off the southern side of the U.S.V.I. are much smaller and less numerous.

The best time of year to fly the 1,100 miles from Miami and charter a boat to get in on the blue marlin action at St. Thomas is usually from July through October. While the largest crewed charter fleet in the world exists here, early reservations are still prudent. Full day rates vary from about $400 to $800, depending on the boat size, equipment and service provided.

Yellowtail snapper and grouper can also be taken in the U.S.V.I. The reefs holding such fish are often in waters that are not flat. They don't call these the windward islands for nothing. Not many people fly to these islands and pay charter captains to anchor over bottom fish, when the offshore action is so good, though.

There are also tarpon to catch here if you want to pursue them. Most are caught around docks at night and from shore during the spring. Bonefish are plentiful on the limited flats and coral reefs around the islands, but they too are usually overlooked by visitors. Local interest is negligible and there are few guides in the U.S.V.I. that know anything about such a fishery.

With proper catch-and-release care, the blue marlin fishery off St. Thomas and the U.S. Virgin Islands should remain viable for years to come. Right now, it is the most consistent in the Caribbean.

27

VIRGINS AND WRECKS

Excellent Weather, Marine Life And Wrecks Make This A Must-See, Says Tim

Perhaps one of the reasons I'm so fond of St. Thomas is that it was one of my first ventures into the Caribbean many years ago. I found it an ideal 'foreign' location for someone making his first trip out of the country.

Most importantly, if you are traveling with a non-diving spouse who is interested in seeing what the sport is all about but is not yet committed to getting certified, St. Thomas is ideal. Resort courses virtually originated here; after just a few hours of pool training your partner will be ready to join you on a shallow reef dive.

Coki Beach not only offers some of the prettiest views on the island, its normally calm waters have long been a natural swimming pool for resort courses. In fact, this is where many of the first-time cruise ship novices make their first plunge in water that varies from 12 to 18 feet deep.

For experienced pros, St. Thomas has some very exciting sites. Frenchman's Cap, a mile south of St. Thomas, received its name from the large rock that looks like Napoleon's three-cornered hat. Good visibility usually prevails, from 75 to 100 feet. Marine life can be excellent. Often you'll be able to find nurse sharks sleeping on the sand bottom and schools of big pelagics swimming by. Grouper, rays, turtles and snapper are typical residents. In February and March, it's possible to hear humpback whales in the area. On occasion, a few divers have even been fortunate enough to swim here with the magnificent creatures.

Two protruding rocks just a half-mile out known as Cow and Calf are named after a pair of humpbacks spotted here many years ago. The larger rock, Cow, is peppered with incredibly lined tunnels and arches, a submarine wallpaper of bright sponges and small corals. One tunnel, known as Champagne Cork because of the way the surge pops you through the bottlenecked opening, is often filled with silver minnows. This can be a terrific location for a night dive.

At Thatch Cay just off Coki Beach, tarpon and turtles are frequently sighted near the maze of tunnels and ledges that cut through the island. Copper sweepers and orange corals furnish an unforgettable panorama inside some of the stone corridors. However, there can be a strong cross-current here at times which may make diving difficult if not impossible.

East of Thatch Cay are a chain of islands--Grass, Mingo, Congo and Lovango Cays and Carval Rock--that offer more good diving. The sand chute between Congo and Lovango has been dubbed "The Yellow Brick Road" because of all the exciting possibilities: big rays in the sand, abundant sand dollars and sea biscuits, and eagle rays. Carval Rock, often beset by strong current, attracts tremendous schools of fry, which in turn attract big fish like dolphin and tarpon. You can also find a good forest of elkhorn coral here.

Little Buck Island, excellent for both snorkeling and diving, was once used by astronauts attempting to feel the sensation of weightlessness. The wreck of the "Cartanser" is located here. Other wrecks around St. Thomas include the "HMS Packet" which ran aground at Packet Rock and the "Major General Rogers," on the bottom at 70 feet and another popular night dive.

St John

Like St. Thomas, St. John has some spectacular beaches. The best known is at Trunk Bay, whose underwater snorkeling trail with its red, white and blue markers isn't nearly as well known (or crowded) as the Buck Island trail at St. Croix. Although far fewer people ever visit St. John, the island still supports four scuba operators, a testimony to the quality of the diving.

For diving, St. John operators use some of the same locations as their St. Thomas counterparts. Lameshur Bay was the base for the pioneering Tektite underwater habitats positioned in 50 feet of water. Clear water and abundant marine life are what made this an ideal location for the experiments.

An unforgettable panorama exists inside some of the wrecks.

Steven's Cay just outside Cruz Bay is noted for its lobsters, nurse sharks and pillar coral. A coral amphitheater forms a kind of fish bowl as well as a protected place to dive when the current is running. Dever's Canyon, in just 50 feet of water, also boasts its share of nurse sharks and lobsters hiding under the colorful overhangs. In more open water, look for the resident puffer fish and the goodly assortment of sponges.

Since St. Thomas and St. John are such close neighbors, it's convenient to escape from one to the other to experience the vastly different lifestyles of each. That, coupled with the superb diving shared by each, is a unique feature to makes this already alluring region all the more attractive.

St Croix

Buck Island Reef National Monument, two miles north of St. Croix, is probably the most visited and best known snorkeling/diving site anywhere in the Virgins. Under the protection of the park service since 1961, it is visited many times daily by excursion boats from Christiansted.

Underwater markers in the shape of grave headstones mark Buck Island's famed underwater trail, which is suffering from both its popularity and the effects of Hugo. The shallowest corals show obvious signs of damage and some were even uprooted, but the schools of fish happily remain.

Christiansted-based divers have virtually the entire northeast coast as their playground, with reefs and steep drops bordering the entire shoreline. As a result, there are scores of dive sites and new ones are being found all the time. In addition, several wrecks have been deliberately sunk for variety.

Lots of tropicals frequent the Salt River Canyon East Slope, which also enjoys good sponge growth. The dropoff begins at just under 40 feet and plummets to either 1,000 feet, 6,000 feet or 12,000 feet, depending on who you listen to. Personally, I always enjoy hearing such widely varying estimates because the emphasis on depth somehow implies that the steeper and deeper the drop, the better the diving, which isn't necessarily true; and it's not likely any of us are ever going to see the bottom.

The West Slope of Salt River Canyon offers black coral as shallow as 80 feet and deepwater gorgonians are common. The Salt River area also happens to be a very historic region, where Columbus came ashore for fresh water in 1493 and named the island Santa Cruz or Holy Island.

Moving more westward, the walls at Cane and Davis Bay come is so close they can be dived from shore. In fact, many locals do dive Cane Bay from the beach. I made a dive at Davis Bay with Blue Paradise Scuba at the Carambola Beach Resort and Golf Club. We swam out 150 yards, our BC's inflated, which gave us a fine view of Carambola's very picturesque beach.

Before recent hurricanes, Davis Bay must have been an exceptional dive, with numerous coral canyons leading to the dropoff starting at about 40 feet. Unfortunately, many of the corals are still covered with sediment, so that sections of reef are dying. At the same time, others are coming back with remarkable patches of bright color, and the variety of fish provided some interesting photo opportunities.

The colorful variety of encrusted corals provide interesting photo opportunities.

Mile Marker Watersports and Dive St. Croix (a combined operation located in the King Christian Hotel complex) showed me several very photogenic wrecks on their weekly Sunday run to far-flung Butler Bay, actually quite close to Frederiksted. At 103 feet down on the 177-foot long "Rosaomaira," one of the divemasters emptied a tank into a large air pocket at the vessel's stern near the prop. One by one we came up, took our regulators out and discovered how difficult it is to be macho at 103 feet when your voice sounds like Donald Duck.

The interior of the wheelhouse has some good encrusting sponge growth that is evident only with a light. It's also possible to penetrate a small way into the wreck, including a head still with toilet and a galley (kitchen) with all its crockery and a floating egg carton. However, it's very easy to silt up the inside and divers must crawl ahead with their hands and not use their fins.

The "Northwind" is a 75-foot ocean tug used as a film prop. The colorful, sponge-encrusted anchor provides excellent photo opportunities, as does the wheel house. Sharks and Southern sting rays are often spotted here. An old underwater habitat is just a short swim from the "Northwind," and many divers start there and finish at the tug, where the boat is anchored.

I did not see the "Suffolk Maid," a 144-foot steel hulled North Sea trawler that sits upright in 60 feet of water. However, the superstructure was removed from the "Suffolk Maid" before it was scuttled, so resident and passing schools of fish are the main interest.

The old Frederiksted pier is tops for macro photography. However, all of the old pier is underwater, the section closest to the surface having been removed by Hugo. Besides eels, puffers and octopus, the marine life on the pilings still includes those legendary sea horses that Frederiksted has long been famous for. A superb night dive. Cruzan Divers, located in Frederiksted right on the waterfront, dives the pier often and also frequently visits the wrecks in Butler Bay.

28

PICTURESQUE RETREATS

The British Virgin Islands are located just 60 miles east of Puerto Rico in the Northern Caribbean. You won't find swinging nightclubs and high rise hotels here. You will find, however, sweeping white sand beaches, privacy and informality. The three main islands are Tortola, Peter Island and Virgin Gorda. Others include Anegada, Cooper, Norman and Jost Van Dyke islands. They are all grouped around the Sir Francis Drake Channel.

The BVI's, adjacent to the U.S. Virgin Islands, are an extremely picturesque group. Many are mountainous and during the early summer rainy season look lushly vegetated. When it's dry, they change to a deep brown and become more desert-like, yet palms, mangoes, cactus, loblolly, frangipani, hibiscus and bougainvillea all thrive here.

The British Virgins are the kind of islands most people wouldn't mind owning and retreating to. Except for the occasional storm, temperatures are almost perfect: between 77-85 degrees in winter, only 80-90 during summer, with temps dropping about 10 degrees each evening. Water temperatures are just as ideal, in the 80s during summer, only slightly cooler in winter.

It's a totally water-oriented community with little in the way of nightlife or other social opportunities. After dark activities, if they don't take place underwater, are confined either to the hotels or the sailboat decks. Just as for the pirates of old, the BVI's are mainly a place for total escape.

All flights to the British Virgin Islands connect through St. Thomas in the U.S. Virgin Islands or San Juan, Puerto Rico. American Eagle flies several times daily from San Juan into Beef Island, which is connected by bridge to Tortola and is just a short drive from Road Town's ferry docks. The American Eagle flights are designed to connect conveniently with other American flights that use San Juan as a hub. This is, by far, the most convenient route.

Visitors arriving by air in St. Thomas can take an inter-island flight to Tortola, then a short cab ride to the ferry docks at Road Town. Or, you can board the ferry to Tortola in St. Thomas, and arrive at the same docks in Road Town where ferry connections can be made to Peter Island and Virgin Gorda. You can also take an inter-island flight from St. Thomas into Spanish Town on Virgin Gorda. Small planes can also land on Anegada Island for those staying at Anegada Reef Resort.

U.S. visitors need only a passport or voter's registration card as proof of citizenship, and return tickets. Even in the BVI's the U.S. Dollar is the official currency. Major credit cards are accepted in many places, but no personal checks. Temperatures usually stay within the 77-85 degree range in the winter and 80-90 F in the summer. At night, temperatures may drop around ten degrees.

Because most inter-island flights have limited space, the amount of luggage is more important than what you bring. With its British heritage, dress is a little more formal at the beautiful, upscale resorts like Peter Island and Biras Creek, which means slacks and light jackets for men in the evening. Both accommodations are superb, offering delicious meals, the ultimate in service, and even fishing and diving packages. Other hotels and resorts are more casual, with shorts and T-shirts suitable for the evening. No bare male chests or female midriffs are allowed in commercial areas and nudity is punishable by law.

On a clear day you can see virtually all of the Virgin Islands from Tortola, the largest of the BVI. Mount Sage, a National Park, rises to 1,780 feet and traces of a rain forest are found on its slopes. Road Town is the capital, and the island has a population of less than 10,000.

The second largest island is Virgin Gorda, dominated by a 1,300-foot mountain peak on its northern half, while its southern half is flat with giant boulders appearing at almost every turn. The island is known for "The Baths," a unique rock formation and popular picnic and boating destination. It is a popular stop for both yachtsmen and divers. Its neighbor, Anegada Island, is third in size. Only 28 feet above sea level, it can barely be seen on the horizon when approaching by boat. Peter Island, home of Peter Island Hotel and Yacht Harbour, and Jost Van Dyke, are other popular destinations. Except for Tortola, most British Virgin Islands are secluded and offer fewer accommodations than you

Numerous secluded coves around the British Virgin Islands are beautiful, scenic stops for yachtsmen and divers.

might expect. But what they lack in accommodation choices, they more than make up in service and quality.

For complete travel, dive, sportfishing and hotels/resorts information, contact The British Virgin Islands Tourist Board, 370 Lexington Ave., Suite 511, New York, NY 10017 or 1686 Union St., San Francisco, CA 94123. Toll free nationwide except Calif. (800) 922-4876. In Calif., (800) 922-4873.

29

ROYAL BLUE BATTLEFIELD

Larry Enjoys Fishing With A Backdrop Of Mountainous Terrain Jutting From The Emerald Waters

"Hook up!" shouted Captain Dennis Steele of the "Escape" over his CB. That call, just 15 minutes into the fishing day, got our attention aboard the "Sea Eagle."

We peered over the 3-foot seas at the nearby boat and sure enough, their angler was strapped in the fighting chair hanging onto a bent rod. Captain Glynn Loftin turned the 65-foot Hatteras Convertible toward the action just 400 yards away. The ploy of moving near an apparent feeding "school" of blues had worked for him on the two previous days.

"Sea Eagle" owner, Don Stallings, and his wife, Billie, moved anxiously across the cockpit toward the 80 pound Internationals. As our sportfisherman pulled adjacent to the battle ensuing near the transom of the "Escape," a "pod" of blues appeared in our baits. The first marlin seemed most interested in the small teaser tethered from the right rigger. It slapped at the artificial a couple of times while Stallings quickly moved the plastic skirt and ballyhoo rig from the right flat line up to the action.

While Don worked on trying to entice that 100 pound blue, another broke from the pod and struck the left rigger bait. It missed, but Billie, manning the rod, moved it back and forth to provide additional action. Another blue then moved on the right rigger bait, and the three all trying to eat created chaos in the cockpit. The latter charge became a solid hook up and Don grabbed for that rod.

Adding to the confusion of the activity was the appearance of two more blues in the baits during the course of the fight. As the mates wound in the right teaser, another blue moved on it. The two fishermen already had their hands full so that fish escaped. The ultimate, a double on blue marlin, did occur, though, and it was the Stalling's first double ever. The rare action was also the first that I had witnessed.

All the blues seemed to be traveling in a school of similar sized fish, around 100 pounds. For the "Sea Eagle," the double was two of 12 blues that they tagged and released during four days of fishing off Virgin Gorda in the British Virgin Islands. Such results are rare for all sportfishermen, but at a newly "discovered" spot, called the South Drop, exceptional catches have been the rule.

Artificial lures, in black and pink, and ballyhoo with red rubber skirts entice many of the blues at the South Drop. Black Hawaiian Eyes preceding ballyhoo, and both mackerel and squid are utilized by knowledgeable captains. All are attractive to the blues. Larger baits are normally used by local captains when specifically chasing big blues during the late summer months.

The blues off the South Drop seemed to bite close to the boat. The aggressive fish will usually strike the flat line baits and often come into the teasers. On windy days, the rough seas will find the marlin striking further back on baits presented off the riggers. The trade winds in the BVI can increase and seas may average ten feet and higher during tropical depressions.

Finding Blue Water Species

Add to the great marlin fishing angling action for other species such as tuna, wahoo and dolphin, and the trip that won't be forgotten awaits. Fishing there is seldom hyped, even by some excellent resort hideaways on Virgin Gorda and Peter Island. Both are near the overlooked fishing.

For the billfisherman, the Barracuda Banks, a series of sea mounts about 12 miles off Virgin Gorda, offers an option. Round Rock, between Peter Island and Virgin Gorda, is another less-pressured option that offers depths of 400 feet alongside a dropoff. Marlin up to 200 pounds and sailfish up to 75 pounds have been caught there.

The dropoff continues gradually all the way to the Sea Mound about 10 miles southeast of Round Rock. Larger blues are often caught off that underwater structure. A current off the Round Rock dropoff normally moves northeast but can shift to the

The South Drop, produces exceptional blue marlin catches, and sportfishermen often proudly display numerous release flags.

southeast. At the Sea Mound, the current will run southerly and vary directionally, depending on the moon.

A better option exists, however, for those anglers based out of Virgin Gorda or Peter Island. The area just east of Anegada, called Horseshoe Reef, is where the South Drop lies, and a better blue marlin area in this world would be hard to find.

Anegada's barrier reef system there is twice as long as the flat island and is the second largest in the western hemisphere. Over 300 shipwrecks have taken place on those skirting reefs, but a few miles out the bottom drops quickly, tapering from 20 to over 200 fathoms. Along its rock-hard bottom lie numerous peaks and humps. Huge schools of flying fish sail the surface, and masses of squid roam the topography below.

Discovering Coveys Of Blues

It was the South Drop area where the Biras Creek International Team Fishing Tournament established several record catches a couple of years ago. On the first day alone, nine boats caught and released 27 blue marlin from the area off Horseshoe Reef. Over the four-day event, 87 blues were caught and released, giving the teams a 9.6 fish per boat average! That's unheard of in marlin tournament circles.

The "Escape" won the event with 19 blue marlin. The boat, with two anglers aboard, caught and released seven fish on the first day, and had 34 blue marlin bites in the exciting tournament. The best marlin fishing of their lives finally occurred after years of fishing throughout the Bahamas and Caribbean islands. The most blues that they had ever caught prior to visiting Virgin Gorda (in a four day tournament) was three.

While many of the blues there are small, some large fish exist. One disappointed angler fought one for over one hour before losing it at the stern. The fish, judged to be about 450 pounds, was hooked in the jaw outside of the mouth. The mate had the leader several times, but when the gaff struck only the dorsal fin, the fish pulled the hook.

"We have not seen triple hitters and quads anywhere else," said one experienced marlin chaser. "During the tournament, there were coveys of blues coming up, just like sailfish or white marlin."

For big blues, local captains suggest fishing in late September or October. Captain Dale Wheatley's largest taken aboard his "Sundance" was a blue marlin that weighed 918 pounds at the Virgin Gorda Yacht Harbor. In one three day stretch during the summer of 1988, he caught seven blue marlin. Moored just down from Murdering Hole Bay at nearby Blunder Bay, the charter boat is one of the few handy to the South Drop.

Charters offering both half day and full day fishing excursions to nearby dropoffs operate out of Peter Island, Virgin Gorda and Tortola. The winds often kick up in the afternoon, but the occasional rains are not normally limited to a certain time of day. Weather shouldn't impact the marlin fishing around the BVI.

The BVIs are also a perfect destination to charter a sailboat or sportsfishing boat with crew, or captain your own boat (if you have the necessary experience). Rates vary depending on size of vessel and whether crew is needed. Weekly rates in the winter can average 40% more than during the off-season in the summer. You supply your own food.

The flats off nearby Mosquito Island average about one foot of depth and are teeming with bonefish.

Light Tackle Bones

The bonefishing off nearby Mosquito Island is tremendous. The flats averaging about one foot of depth there, in fact, are teaming with bonefish. Other bonefish have been taken from the mangrove shallows in front of the marina and along the flats near the service docks. Schools will create "muds" as they move through the area feeding on crabs along the bottom. The island of Anegada has a huge flats area and offers excellent bonefishing.

Marlin anglers Charlie Campbell and Doc Stewart of the "Escape," went bonefishing in their "flats-rigged" dingy several times in between fishing a marlin tournament. They averaged about 10 fish per 3-hour jaunt. The two-some used shrimp on spinning equipment, rather than the flies they had brought along, since the winds were significant. Their bonefish were large, 7 to 10 pounds.

I accompanied them to one place that must have had 150 bonefish in one bunch. We caught several and Campbell even caught an 18 pound permit there. With both light and heavy tackle sportfishing options and relatively easy access, the beautiful isles should be on any sportsman's travel itinerary.

169

30

PIRATE TREASURES BELOW

Tim Tangles With A Famous Movie Star And Gets Wrecked

The British Virgin Islands abound with so many colorful stories it's difficult to detect fact from fable. For instance, it was on Dead Chest Island that Blackbeard marooned 15 of his buccaneers with only a bottle or rum and a cutlass. It's not clear how many survived, but enough to commemorate their ordeal in the famous "Yo-Ho-Ho and a Bottle of Rum" song. And Robert Louis Stevenson's "Treasure Island" is here, though it's called Norman Island after a pirate whose treasure is believed still buried there.

But probably most famous of all is the legendary wreck of the "Rhone," a movie star that has captivated divers from the world over.

The "Rhone," along with actress Jacqueline Bisset's wet T-shirt, were the high points of an otherwise fairly forgettable movie of over a decade ago called "The Deep." Yet the colorfully encrusted, 310-foot "Rhone" was revealed as something truly rare: a sunken ship that looks just the way Hollywood (and divers) publicize them.

The "Rhone" is only one of scores of documented wrecks that lie along the Sir Francis Drake Channel, one of the world's best sailing grounds. Then why all the wrecks? Primarily due to pirates or hurricanes or foundering on an uncharted reef system that today is so well mapped even first time sailors in the region have no trouble. It's so safe, in fact, that over 1,000 rag-powered vessels are available for charter throughout the year, some of which specialize in diving as well as sailing.

Without doubt, the favorite dive spot in all the BVI's is the "Rhone," a grand old lady who is keeping her shape magnificently since her demise well over a century ago. It's been said some unfortunates are destined to be more famous in death than life, and that certainly was the fate of the steel hulled "Rhone" built in London in 1865. And although the "Rhone" hasn't been above the surface since she sank in 1867, thanks to "The Deep" she has been seen by more people than almost any other ship in history.

Although already popular among more adventurous divers, her movie fame was a real bonus. Realizing what a treasure they had on their hands, the BVI government declared her a national monument shortly after the film's release. That meant hands off to salvagers so that the thousands of divers who pilgrimage here annually will see her intact.

What makes the "Rhone" such an ideal dive is most of her hull resembles its original shape--not a pretzeled mass of twisted beams. And she is in fairly shallow water, resting between 30-80 feet. It helps to know a little of the "Rhone's" history before visiting her. The way she met her end explains why she is so well preserved. Further, it's unusual for such a popular wreck to be so well documented.

The "Rhone" was an unusual ship for her day. Weighing 2,738 tons, she was powered by both steam and sail. Two large steel masts sported square-rigged sails which would enable her to make port in case of an engine breakdown or fuel (coal) shortage. Her 500-hp steam engine, which drove a single-screw iron propeller with a top speed of 14 knots, was considered a great improvement over the traditional side or paddle-wheels.

The "Rhone" was specifically designed for transatlantic passage, carrying mail, general cargo and only a few passengers. She was returning from her 10th voyage when she was sunk by a fierce hurricane that also sank 75 other ships, caused $2 million in damage and killed 500 people. Over a fourth of that death toll came from the "Rhone" alone.

It happened Oct. 29, 1867. The ship was taking on supplies off Peter Island (close to where it now rests) when the ship's barometer fell and the sky suddenly blackened. The storm hit quickly, catching the ship unprepared. The anchor began to drag and for an hour the crew ran the engine at full power to hold position. Unexpectedly, a lull came in the storm as the hurricane's eye passed over, and the captain steered for open sea where he thought the ship would have a better chance of riding out the storm.

The ship had almost reached open water, passing between Salt and Dead Chest Islands, when the ferocious winds returned, actually

Many shallower regions are good for snorkelers. You can see lots of pillar coral and fans.

driving the ship backward onto the tip of Salt Island. One of the propeller blades sheared and the ship soon went down. She broke in half, with 150 feet of the bow settling into 80 feet of water. The stern slid into only 30 feet, part of it above water; this section was gradually scattered over several acres of bottom in the passing years, but the bow remained unmoved and intact.

Of the 129 officers and crew and 16 passengers, 123 died. At that time, it was perhaps the worst maritime tragedy in history.

My most recent dive on the "Rhone" couldn't have contrasted more dramatically to that fateful October day of long ago. The sun was intensely bright, the water almost glassy calm. Ironically, the "Baskin' in the Sun" dive boat had to come to Peter Island--the "Rhone's" last anchorage--to pick me up. Peter Island, a 1200-acre privately owned island, has now become an exclusive hideaway where such celebrities as Robert Redford and Paul McCartney frequent. However, even mere mortals like myself are also welcome in these casually swank surroundings in some of the more reasonably priced motel-style rooms.

Peter Island, like many of the resorts, doesn't have its own dive boat but contracts with an operator. In this instance, Baskin' in the Sun in Tortola, just a short hop across the Sir Francis Drake Channel. This sort of procedure, known as rendezvous diving, is common in the BVI's, especially for those exploring by sailboat. Just by letting an operator know in advance where you'll be anchored, they'll pick you up and take you off for a dive for a few hours or bring you a fresh set of tanks or even full gear if you need it. Dive shops here tend to be well equipped, almost as good as the States.

Most dives on the "Rhone" are two tanks, starting deep at the bow, then moving to the shallow stern. Considering all the publicity the ship has received, your first glimpse of the bow may be a disappointment. From a distance, the huge overturned hull looks about as interesting as the bottom of a capsized canoe. The real treat is the ship's interior, which has easy access at many points.

Swimming inside close to the bottom, the steel girders above are like the exposed beam of a chapel. But these supports are alive with encrusted sponges and orange corals. Hovering behind and over the beams are large schools of fish, closely packed together, which seem to fade gradually into infinity. In this shadowy place, where the only sound is your breathing, there's no feeling of a tomb or the catastrophe that occurred. But while there may be no sense of foreboding or uneasiness, there is the somber atmosphere of a museum or library, a place where one should reflect on the lessons of the past.

Moving through the interior, you may experience the unusual sensation of true weightless the way the astronauts do. In the ocean, you are rarely enclosed on all sides. The cocoon of the "Rhone's" hull supplies a constant reference to emphasize how you are indeed defying gravity.

On the shallow second dive at the stern, the most interesting remain is the great propeller. Gazing down from the surface as another diver grips one of the blades, the force of the fatal hurricane winds become tangible. The prop greatly dwarfs any diver, seemingly more than adequate to combat the sea. Tragically, it wasn't.

What else in the BVI's can begin to compare to the "Rhone?" On a less grandiose scale is the wreck of the "Chikuzen," a 286-foot refrigeration ship that sank in the early 1980s. It's become a huge fish attractor since there isn't anything else in the immediate area to draw marine life. A host of pelagics typically visit the wreck: rays, horseye jacks, African pompano, permit and occasionally reef

The Baths are a well-known sailing and snorkeling site near Virgin Gorda.

sharks. Barracudas often hang close to the surface, then drop to patrol the wreck with divers.

The caves off Norman ("Treasure") Island, where gold coins supposedly were found not long ago, are filled with a more reliable treasure, a storehouse of glassy sweepers and sergeant majors. The curtain of fish there can be incredibly dense: the glassy sweepers number well into the thousands.

The Indians, close to both Norman and Peter Islands, consists of four large rocks emerging from the ocean bottom to a height of 90 feet. Greatest depth is only 50 feet with many shallower regions good for snorkelers. You can see lots of pillar coral and fans and a cave filled with silvery copper sweepers. Or try Painted Walls, a series of long surge canyons loaded with colorful encrusted life, hence the name. Or Blonde Rocks, which receives its name from the mustard-colored fire coral, home to a large schools of grunts and more copper sweepers.

Blonde Rock is a pinnacle between Dead Chest and Salt Island that rises from the 60-foot bottom to within 15 feet of the surface. On good days, the rock ledges, overhangs and tunnels are home to hordes of reef fish. Santa Monica Rock, a pinnacle like Blonde

175

Rock, is on the outer edge of the island chain, which makes it a good place to spot deep water fish like spotted eagle rays. The pinnacle itself starts at 100 feet and rises to within 10 feet of the surface.

Or try The Chimney at Virgin Gorda, a popular fish feeding/ photographing site, or to the most remote reef of all--Anegada Reef, probably the greatest ship killer in all the Caribbean. Over 300 wrecks are known to have piled up on Anegada Reef since the 1500s. Anegada Island has no large rolling hills but rises only 28 feet at its highest point. Surrounded by a great fringing reef that extends for miles, sailors in the past never anticipated the devastating reefs since they could spot no nearby land mass to warn them. Divers still find plenty of ballast stones or iron debris. This is too far to dive from Tortola or Peter Island, so divers usually stay in the area and are normally served by an excellent operation, Kilbride's Underwater Tours at Saba Rock.

Filming custom underwater video for individuals or dive groups is a service many of the dive operators provide. Some dive shops will arrange for an underwater photographer to follow you around, shoot a roll of 36 exposures, and hand the slides over to you at the end of the dive.

Most dive packages are for hotels in Tortola and Virgin Gorda. Prices are per person per week, double occupancy and usually feature two tanks a day, with sometimes unlimited diving. Most quoted rates do not include the automatically added 7% hotel tax or 10% service charge. You can also arrange to stay at a guest house and sign up to dive at your convenience.

Outside of diving, Virgin Gorda is probably the most interesting of the all the British islands due to the huge granite rock formations at its southwest point. The boulders seem to have been thrown atop one another haphazardly, creating numerous caves, including one spot where the waves have washed away the sand to create big saltwater pools called The Baths. Understandably, this is a favorite anchorage/picnic site.

If you're looking for Caribbean isles the way you've dreamed of them, try the British Virgins. The diving may live up to your fantasies, too.

APPENDICES

APPENDIX A

Tourism Contacts

Bahamas Tourist Office
255 Alhambra Cir.#425
Coral Gables, FL 33134
305/224-4860

Bermuda Dept.of Tourism
310 Madison Ave. #201
New York, NY 10017

BVI Tourist Board
370 Lexington Ave.
New York, NY 10017
212/696-0400

Cayman Islands Dept. of Tourism
250 Catalonia Ave.
Coral Gables, FL 33134
305/444-6551

Jamaica Tourist Board
1320 S. Dixie Hwy. #1100
Coral Gables, FL 33146
305/665-0557

Mexico Gov. Tourist Office
405 Park Ave.
New York, NY 10022
212/755-7212

Puerto Rico Tourism
Office
200 SE 1st St. #903
Miami, FL 33131
305/381-8915

Turks & Caicos Tourist
Board
425 Madison Ave.
New York, NY 10017
800/441-4419

U.S.V.I. Div. of Tourism
2655 Le Jeune Rd. #907
Coral Gables, FL 33134
305/442-7200

To verify the information within, the above agencies were contacted prior to publication. We appreciate the information received from those who responded.

WRITE US!

By the way, if our books have helped you be more productive in your outdoor endeavors, we'd like to hear from you. Let us know which book or series has strongly benefited you and how it has aided your success or enjoyment.

We might be able to use the information in a future book. Such information is also valuable to our planning future titles and expanding on those already available.

Simply write to: Larry Larsen, Publisher, Larsen's Outdoor Publishing, 2640 Elizabeth Place, Lakeland, FL 33813.

We appreciate your comments!

FISHING & HUNTING RESOURCE DIRECTORY

If you are interested in more productive fishing and hunting trips, then this info is for you!

Larsen's Outdoor Publishing is the publisher of several quality Outdoor Libraries - all informational-type books that focus on how and where to catch America's most popular sport fish, hunt America's most popular big game or travel to productive or exciting destinations.

The perfect-bound, soft-cover books include numerous illustrative  graphics, line drawings, maps and photographs. The BASS SERIES LIBRARY and the two HUNTING LIBRARIES are nationwide in scope. The INSHORE SERIES covers coastal areas from Texas to Maryland and foreign waters. The OUTDOOR TRAVEL SERIES covers the most popular fishing and diving destinations in the world. The BASS WATERS SERIES focuses on the top lakes and rivers in the nation's most visited largemouth bass fishing state.

All series appeal to outdoorsmen/readers of all skill levels. The unique four-color cover design, interior layout, quality, information content and economical price makes these books hot sellers in the marketplace. Best of all, you can learn to be more successful in your outdoor endeavors!!

SEE ORDERING INFORMATION ON PAGE 159

THE BASS SERIES LIBRARY
by Larry Larsen

1. FOLLOW THE FORAGE FOR BETTER BASS ANGLING VOL. 1 BASS/PREY RELATIONSHIP

Learn how to determine the dominant forage in a body of water, and you will consistently catch more and larger bass. Whether you fish artificial lures or live bait, your bass stringer will benefit!

2. FOLLOW THE FORAGE FOR BETTER BASS ANGLING VOL. 2 TECHNIQUES

Learn why one lure or bait is more successful than others and how to use each lure under varying conditions. You will also learn highly productive patterns that will catch bass under most circumstances!

3. BASS PRO STRATEGIES

Professional fishermen know how changes in pH, water temperature, color and fluctuations affect bass fishing, and they know how to adapt to weather and topographical variations. Learn from their experience. Your productivity will improve after spending a few hours with this compilation of tactics!

4. BASS LURES - TRICKS & TECHNIQUES

When bass become accustomed to the same artificials and presentations seen over and over again, they become harder to catch. Learn how to rig or modify your lures and develop specific presentation and retrieve methods to spark or renew the interest of largemouth!

5. SHALLOW WATER BASS

Bass spend 90% of their time in the shallows, and you spend the majority of the time fishing for them in waters less than 15 feet deep. Learn specific productive tactics that you can apply to fishing in marshes, estuaries, reservoirs, lakes, creeks and small ponds. You'll likely triple your results!

THE BASS SERIES LIBRARY
by Larry Larsen

6. BASS FISHING FACTS

Learn why and how bass behave during pre- and post-spawn, how they utilize their senses and how they respond to their environment, and you'll increase your bass angling success! This angler's guide to the lifestyles and behavior of the black bass is a reference source never before compiled. It examines how bass utilize their senses to feed. By applying this knowledge, your productivity will increase for largemouth as well as Redeye, Suwannee, Spotted and other bass species.

7. TROPHY BASS

If you're more interested in wrestling with one or two monster largemouth than with a "panfull" of yearlings, then learn what techniques and habitats will improve your chances. This book takes a look at geographical areas and waters that offer better opportunities to catch giant bass, as well as proven methods and tactics for both man made and natural waters. The "how to" information was gleaned from professional guides and other experienced trophy bass hunters.

8. ANGLER'S GUIDE TO BASS PATTERNS

Catch bass every time out by learning how to develop a productive pattern quickly and effectively. Learn the most effective combination of lures, methods and places. Understanding bass movement and activity and the most appropriate and effective techniques to employ will add many pounds of enjoyment to the sport of bass fishing.

9. BASS GUIDE TIPS

Learn the most productive methods of top bass fishing guides in the country and secret techniques known only in a certain region or state that may work in your waters. Special features include shiners, sunfish kites & flies; flippin, pitchin' & dead stickin' rattlin; skippin' & jerk baits; moving, deep, hot & cold waters; fronts, high winds & rain. New approaches for bass angling success!

INSHORE SERIES
by Frank Sargeant

IL1. THE SNOOK BOOK

"Must" reading for anyone who loves the pursuit of this unique sub-tropic species. Every aspect of how you can find and catch big snook is covered, in all seasons and all waters where snook are found.

IL2. THE REDFISH BOOK

Packed with expertise from the nation's leading redfish anglers and guides, this book covers every aspect of finding and fooling giant reds. You'll learn secret techniques revealed for the first time.

IL3. THE TARPON BOOK

Find and catch the wily "silver king" along the Gulf Coast, north through the mid-Atlantic, and south along Central and South American coastlines. Numerous experts share their most productive techniques.

IL4. THE TROUT BOOK - *COMING SOON!*

You'll learn the best seasons, techniques and lures in this comprehensive book.

OUTDOOR TRAVEL SERIES
by M. Timothy O'Keefe and Larry Larsen

A candid guide with inside information on the best charters, time of the year, and other vital recommendations that can make your next fishing and/or diving trip much more enjoyable.

OT1. FISH & DIVE THE CARIBBEAN - Volume 1

Northern Caribbean, including Cozumel, Caymans Bahamas, Virgin Islands and other popular destinations.

OT2. FISH & DIVE THE CARIBBEAN - Volume 2 - *COMING SOON!* Southern Caribbean, including Guadeloupe, Bonaire, Costa Rica, Venezuela and other destinations.

DEER HUNTING LIBRARY
by John E. Phillips

DH1. MASTERS' SECRETS OF DEER HUNTING
Increase your deer hunting success significantly by learning from the masters of the sport. New information on tactics and strategies for bagging deer is included in this book, the most comprehensive of its kind.

DH2. THE SCIENCE OF DEER HUNTING - *COMING SOON!*

TURKEY HUNTING LIBRARY
by John E. Phillips

TH1. MASTERS' SECRETS OF TURKEY HUNTING
Masters of the sport have solved some of the most difficult problems you will encounter while hunting wily longbeards with bows, blackpowder guns and shotguns. Learn 10 deadly sins of turkey hunting and what to do if you commit them.

TH2. OUTSMART TOUGH TURKEYS - *COMING SOON!*

BASS WATERS SERIES
by Larry Larsen

Take the guessing game out of your next bass fishing trip. The most productive bass waters in each region of the state are described in this multi-volume series, including boat ramp information, seasonal tactics, water characteristics and much more. Popular and overlooked lakes, rivers, streams, ponds, canals, marshes and estuaries are clearly detailed with numerous maps and drawings.

BW1. GUIDE TO NORTH FLORIDA BASS WATERS
From Orange Lake north and west.

BW2. GUIDE TO CENTRAL FLORIDA BASS WATERS
From Tampa/Orlando to Palatka.

BW3. GUIDE TO SOUTH FLORIDA BASS WATERS
COMING SOON! - from I-4 to the Everglades.

Save Money on Your Next Outdoor Book!

Because you've purchased a Larsen's Outdoor Publishing Book, you can be placed on our growing list of **preferred customers.**

● You can receive special discounts on our wide selection of Bass Fishing, Saltwater Fishing, Hunting, Outdoor Travel and other economically-priced books written by **our expert authors.**

PLUS...

● **Receive Substantial Discounts for Multiple Book Purchases! And...advance notices on upcoming books!**

Send in your name TODAY to be added to our mailing list

___ Yes, put my name on your mailing list to receive:

1. Advance notice on **upcoming outdoor books.**
2. Special **discount offers.**

Name_____

Address_____

City/State/Zip_____

Send to: Larsen's Outdoor Publishing, Special Offers, 2640 Elizabeth Place, Lakeland, FL 33813

LARSEN'S OUTDOOR PUBLISHING
CONVENIENT ORDER FORM
(All Prices Include Postage & Handling)

BASS SERIES LIBRARY - only $11.95 each or $79.95 for autographed set.

_____ 1. Better Bass Angling - Vol. 1- Bass/Prey Interaction
_____ 2. Better Bass Angling - Vol. 2 - Techniques
_____ 3. Bass Pro Strategies
_____ 4. Bass Lures - Tricks & Techniques
_____ 5. Shallow Water Bass
_____ 6. Bass Fishing Facts
_____ 7. Trophy Bass
_____ 8. Angler's Guide to Bass Patterns
_____ 9. Bass Guide Tips

> **BIG SAVINGS!**
> Order 1 book, discount 5%
> 2-3 books, discount 10%.
> 4 or more books discount 20%.

INSHORE SERIES - only $11.95 each

_____ IL1. The Snook Book
_____ IL2. The Redfish Book
_____ IL3. The Tarpon Book

DEER HUNTING SERIES - only $11.95 each

_____ DH1. Masters' Secrets of Deer Hunting

TURKEY HUNTING SERIES - only $11.95 each

_____ TH1. Masters' Secrets of Turkey Hunting

OUTDOOR TRAVEL SERIES - only $13.95 each

_____ OT1. Fish & Dive the Caribbean Vol 1 - Northern Caribbean

BASS WATERS SERIES - only $14.95 each

_____ BW1. Guide To North Florida Bass Waters
_____ BW2. Guide To Central Florida Bass Waters

NAME _____

ADDRESS _____

CITY_____STATE_____ZIP_____

No. of books ordered _____ x $_____ each =   _____
No. of books ordered _____ x $_____ each =   _____
                      Discount   =   _____

TOTAL ENCLOSED (Check or Money Order) $_____

Copy this page and mail to:
Larsen's Outdoor Publishing, Dept. OT
2640 Elizabeth Place, Lakeland, FL 33813

INDEX

189

191